Blast Off!

Blast Off!

Rocketry for Elementary and Middle School Students

Lee Brattland Nielsen

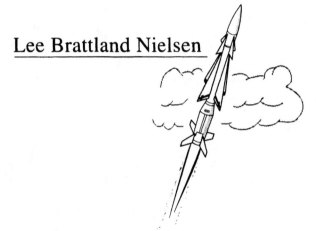

LIBRARIES

U N L I M I T E D

A Member of the Greenwood Publishing Group

Westport, Connecticut • London

Libraries Unlimited
A member of Greenwood Publishing Group, Inc.
88 Post Road West,
Westport, CT 06881
www.lu.com

Production Editor: Stephen Haenel
Copy Editor: Jason Cook
Proofreader: Sharon Cairns Mann
Layout and Design: Michael Florman

Figures 1.1-1.5, 2.1-2.6, 3.3, 3.4, and 7.3 are by National Aeronautics and Space Administration (NASA). Figures 3.1, 5.2, 7.1, and the certificates in Appendix C are by Estes Industries. Figure 3.2 and all photos are by the author.

Library of Congress Cataloging-in-Publication Data

Nielsen, Leona Brattland.
    Blast off! : rocketry for elementary and middle school students / Lee Brattland Nielsen.
        viii, 109p. 22x28 cm.
        Includes bibliographical references and index.
        ISBN 1-56308-438-4
        1. Rocketry--Study and teaching (Elementary) 2. Rocketry--Study and teaching (Secondary) 3. Rocketry--Study and teaching--Simulation methods. I. Title.
    TL782.5.N54 1997
    621.43'56'0712--dc20   96-43789
                                                                        CIP

In order to keep this title in print and available to the academic community, this edition was produced using digital reprint technology in a relatively short print run. This would not have been attainable using traditional methods. Although the cover has been changed from its original appearance, the text remains the same and all materials and methods used still conform to the highest book-making standards.

Contents

v

Preface

Rocketry! What an exciting project for a classroom! The study of rocketry and construction of model rockets provides a motivational and rewarding experience for students of all ages. Rocketry stimulates a desire for continuous learning, inside and outside the classroom.

The study of rockets is a tremendous launching pad for interdisciplinary learning for upper elementary and middle school students. The usual narrow focus of isolated subject matter becomes an integrated approach to teaching math and science, providing students with an opportunity to understand relationships between subjects. Not only do the relevancy and relationship of subjects become apparent, but upper elementary and middle school students also become highly motivated and immersed in their studies of rocketry.

As a special education teacher and resource specialist, I have successfully used the study of rocketry with my special education students, including the emotionally disturbed. The activities surrounding rocketry present endless opportunities for mainstreaming these students. The entire process of building and launching the rockets and presenting a school assembly program results in a true acceptance of special education students by other students. This acceptance in turn promotes a positive self-image and pride of accomplishment. It is this improved attitude toward learning that prompted the writing of this book.

Rocketry lends itself to thematic learning. The linking of concepts and skills around a central theme provides a meaningful learning experience. Studies have shown that learning is most effective not only when it involves active participation, but also when the ideas are relevant to surrounding life situations. The study of rocketry provides such relevancy. The integration of various academic subjects is not only effective but also provides a higher level of understanding in all areas. A thematic unit helps students develop the skills of observation and inquiry. Rocketry as a thematic unit provides students with a successful and rewarding learning experience.

A classroom rocketry project can involve many academic disciplines—science, math, oral communication, composition, reading, art, and even the performing arts. Rocketry as a thematic unit provides a constant reinforcement of concepts and skills across the curriculum. This carry-over of learning stimulates the desire for intellectual investigative growth. I hope that the basics presented in this book will inspire teachers to use the exciting theme of rocketry to enhance their curriculum.

Acknowledgments

I would like to thank Jim Kranich, Manager of Educational Services for Estes Industries, and the people at NASA Jet Propulsion Laboratory, Jet Educational Outreach, for their assistance while writing this book.

Chapter One
The Beginning of Rocketry

Greek and Chinese Origins

A brief history of the beginning of rocketry is an essential starting point for all teachers. As early as 400 B.C., a Roman lawyer and scholar, Aulus Gellius, wrote a story about a Greek named Archytas who made a pigeon of wood. In the story, Archytas mystified the citizens of Tarentum by flying this pigeon. The wooden bird was suspended by wires and propelled by escaping steam. This steam may have been generated in a heated vessel within the wooden body of the pigeon. The steam propellant involved the scientific principle of action-reaction, even though it was not stated as a scientific law until the seventeenth century.

About 300 years after the wooden pigeon, a Greek mathematician, physicist, and engineer, Hero of Alexandria, invented the aeolipile, which, as in the wooden pigeon, used steam as a propellant (see fig. 1.1). He mounted a sphere on top of a water kettle. A fire underneath the kettle turned the water into steam that traveled through two L-shaped pipes on the opposite sides of the sphere. The escaping steam gave thrust to the sphere causing it to rotate.

Fig. 1.1. Aeolipile.

Throughout history, there have been many stories about rocket-like devices, but it is unclear as to when the first true rocket appeared. In the first century A.D., the Chinese developed a simple form of rocket: fire-arrows (see fig. 1.2).

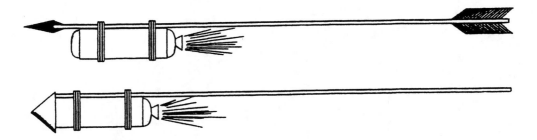

Fig. 1.2. Chinese fire-arrows.

As important as the concept of the rocket is the actual rocket propellant. Late in the third century B.C. the Chinese invented what would later become the first rocket propellant: gunpowder—a mixture of saltpeter (potassium nitrate), sulfur, and charcoal. The Chinese would fill bamboo tubes with this mixture and toss the tubes into fires during religious celebrations and other festivities. It is conjectured that a few of the tubes may not have exploded and, instead, were propelled out of the fire by the gases and sparks of the burning gunpowder.

An old Chinese legend tells the story of one ingenious man who tried to use rockets to fly. It is a story that most children enjoy hearing. A Chinese official, Wan-Hu, made a rocket-powered flying chair. He and his assistants attached two large kites to the chair along with 47 fire-arrow rockets at the back. When it was time for his flight, Wan-Hu sat on the chair and gave the command to light the fire-arrows. The 47 assistants each lit one of the fire-arrows with a torch. Immediately, there was a tremendous roar, and billowing clouds of smoke erupted. After the smoke had cleared, both Wan-Hu and the flying chair were gone! If the event actually did take place, it is probable that both Wan-Hu and the flying chair were blown to pieces. Figure 1.3 shows what Wan-Hu's rocket chair may have looked like.

Fig. 1.3. Legendary Wan-Hu in the rocket chair.

Records from the twelfth century confirm that the Chinese used fire-arrows in the war against the Mongols. At the battle of Kai-Keng, the Chinese drove back the Mongols with "arrows of fire" (see fig. 1.4). Each arrow was a simple, solid-propellant rocket: A tube, filled with gunpowder, was capped on one end; the open end allowed the gas to escape. This tube was attached to a long stick that acted as a guidance system for controlling the direction of flight.

Fig. 1.4. Chinese soldier launching a fire-arrow.

European Rocketry

Following the battle of Kai-Keng, the Mongols produced their own rockets. Mongol rocketry led to an increased interest in rockets throughout Europe. From the thirteenth through the fifteenth centuries, scientists conducted many rocket experiments. Roger Bacon, an English philosopher and scientist, experimented with different forms of gunpowder in an attempt to increase the range of rockets. In France, Jean Froissart discovered that more accurate flights could be achieved by launching rockets through tubes. His idea was the forerunner of the bazooka.

By the sixteenth century, rockets were used less for warfare than previously, though they were still used for fireworks displays. It was Johann Schmidlap, a German fireworks maker, who invented the multistage rocket to lift fireworks to higher altitudes. The first-stage rocket, the larger of the two, carried a sky rocket. When the first-stage rocket burned out, the smaller rocket continued on to higher altitudes while showering the sky with brilliant, glowing cinders. Schmidlap's multistage rocket invention is basic to rocketry today.

The science of rocketry began with Sir Isaac Newton (1642–1727), the English scientist and mathematician. The most popular story about Newton took place in 1666. Newton, always observant and inquisitive, saw an apple fall from a tree while gardening, and he discerned the principle of gravity.

In 1687, Newton published a book, *Philosophiae Naturalis Principia Mathematica*, which described physical principles in nature. He stated three important principles that govern the motion of all objects and which are basic to the performance of all rockets. These three principles, Newton's Laws of Motion, are covered in chapter 2.

Experimenters in Germany and Russia began working with rockets that had a mass (the amount of matter contained in an object) of more than 100 pounds. Some were so powerful that the escaping flames bored deep holes in the ground during lift off.

Colonel William Congreve (1772–1828), an artillery expert, became interested in the use of rockets in warfare. In 1805, this British engineer developed a large, 32-pound rocket that used gunpowder as the propellant. The original range of the rocket was $2\frac{1}{2}$ miles. When it hit the target, the rocket blew up. In 1806, 2,000 of these rockets were fired from small boats in an attack on Boulogne during the Napoleonic Wars; 25,000 rockets were fired against Copenhagen in 1807, and most of the city burned. In the War of 1812, these rockets were used against America. The success of these rockets inspired Francis Scott Key to write about "the rockets' red glare"—writing that would later become "The Star Spangled Banner."

The accuracy of Congreve's rockets was minimal. An Englishman, William Hale, developed a technique called spin stabilization: The exhausting gases struck small vanes at the bottom of the rocket and caused the rocket to spin much like a bullet as it flew through the air, thereby increasing its stability. The United States successfully used the Hale rocket in the war with Mexico in 1846.

The Era of Modern Rocketry

With the reawakened interest in rocketry in the early twentieth century, Konstantin E. Tsiolkovsky (Russian), Hofmann Oberth (Transylvanian German), and Robert H. Goddard (American) worked independently on the fundamental principles of rocket action and their application to escaping the Earth's gravitational field. It was Tsiolkovsky, the Russian school teacher, who stated: "Mankind will not stay on Earth forever but in the pursuit of the world and space, will at first timidly penetrate beyond the limits of the atmosphere and then will conquer all the space around the sun."

As a child, Tsiolkovsky (1857-1935) was inspired by the writings of Jules Verne to pursue an interest in interplanetary travel. Tsiolkovsky, a theoretical engineer, was the first to realize that space travel required propulsion from rockets. Although he never built a rocket, he understood the principle of reaction flight and that the thrust of a rocket came from the ejection of gases, not from the push against an atmosphere. He knew that this thrust would work in a vacuum and that escaping gas would propel the rocket forward in space. He was convinced that the use of a liquid propellant would give more power and range to a rocket than gunpowder and that the speed of a rocket was only limited by the exhaust velocity of escaping gases.

Besides writing many articles, Tsiolkovsky also wrote books about space exploration, including *Dreams of Earth and Sky* and *Outside the Earth*. He wrote his last book, *On the Moon*, the year he died. It was a fictional account of lunar explorers. Tsiolkovsky has been called the Father of Space Travel as well as the Father of Modern Astronautics.

Dr. Robert H. Goddard (1882–1945), an American scientist, is considered the Father of Modern Rocketry. In his autobiography, he wrote about an incident that occurred when he was 17 years old. He had climbed a cherry tree to trim the branches. As he looked down, he pondered that it would be wonderful if one could ascend towards the planets and look down on Earth. He was inspired to achieve his vision—space travel. The cherry tree incident was so important in shaping his life that he celebrated it as his anniversary.

Goddard's research covered all aspects of rocketry, and he conducted many experiments. Results of his tests indicated that a rocket operates better in a vacuum than in air, which was an uncommon idea at that time. He also stated that multistage rockets could achieve greater heights and escape Earth's gravity.

Goddard's earliest experiments involved solid-propellant rockets. Working with solid-propellant rockets convinced him that a rocket could be better propelled with a liquid propellant. However, liquid propellants would be more difficult to use because fuel, oxygen tanks, turbines, and combustion chambers would be needed. On March 16, 1926, Goddard launched the first liquid-fueled rocket, which flew for $2\frac{1}{2}$ seconds, climbed $12\frac{1}{2}$ meters, and landed 56 meters away in a cabbage patch. By today's standards, this first flight may not be impressive, but it was the forerunner of a new era in rocket flight.

As early as 1920, Hermann Oberth (1894–1989), a German mathematician and physicist, foresaw manned space flight. In 1923, Oberth wrote a book, *Rockets into Outer Space*, about travel in space. His writings inspired an increased interest in space travel, and many rocket societies were formed throughout the world. Oberth was a pioneer in the development of liquid-fueled rockets and conceived the idea that interplanetary travel would be possible with liquid-fueled rockets.

The development of rocketry continues. From Aulus Gellius's wooden pigeon to the achievement of manned space flight, the imaginings of yesteryear have matured into visions for the future. To quote Goddard: "It is difficult to say what is impossible, for the dream of yesterday is the hope of today and the reality of tomorrow."

Rocketry and Space Science Today

Today's rocketry and space sciences have been built on the experiences of many pioneers in rocketry. Their dreams, scientific discoveries, and theories have led directly to the continuing advances that are being made in the fields of aeronautics, life science, and spacecraft technology.

Wernher von Braun (1912-1977) is credited as the inventor of the first successful long-range liquid-propelled ballistic missile. Von Braun developed this long-range missile for the German army to use during World War II. The V-2 came into use too late to affect the course of events of the war, as the Germans were already in retreat. After the war, von Braun came to the United States where he continued his work at White Sands Proving Grounds in New Mexico and the Redstone Arsenal in Alabama. Von Braun was instrumental in the development of Jupiter C, a two-stage rocket that made possible America's first satellite launch.

In October 1957, the Soviet Union launched Sputnik I, the first artificial satellite. It orbited the earth every 96 minutes 17 seconds. A month later, another satellite, Sputnik II, was launched carrying a dog named Laika. Soon the United States launched five satellites and three lunar probes that provided scientists with information about regions 70,000 miles away. The space age was here.

While satellite launches increased in frequency, interest and research turned to manned space flight. On April 12, 1961, it became a reality. Yuri Gagarin, a Soviet cosmonaut, became the first person to leave the Earth's atmosphere and enter space in a 108-minute long, one-orbit flight. In May, the Freedom 7 carried American Alan B. Shepard Jr. in a 15-minute orbital flight in space. After that, work began on developing more powerful boosters leading to many other manned space flights. In 1962, von Braun began working on the Saturn, which would eventually be capable of launching spacecraft to the moon. The Saturn V rocket generated 9 million pounds of thrust. This thrust enabled the Saturn V to launch a 150-ton payload into orbit around the moon. Saturn V was 36-stories tall; the bottom stage was so large it had to be transported by barge.

Saturn V launched Apollo 11, which sent astronauts Neil Armstrong, Edwin Aldrin Jr., and Michael Collins to the moon. The landing of the Apollo on the moon on July 20, 1969, was one of the greatest achievements of the United States. When Neil Armstrong stepped from the Apollo lunar module, he announced to the world: "That's one small step for a man; one giant leap for mankind."

In the early 1970s, rocketry science was refocused on the challenge of providing a place for people to work and live in space. Skylab was America's first space station. It was a modified empty third stage of the Saturn V launch vehicle. This space station provided a place for astronauts to live and work for long periods of time. America's first manned space station, Skylab 1, was launched on May 25, 1973. Astronauts worked for 28 days on this mission. Following several other launches, the final Skylab, 3, was launched on November 16, 1974.

Many tests of industrial and biological processes for manufacturing products were conducted on Skylab. Advanced knowledge about human biochemical changes in space was gained. The astronauts on Skylab and the cosmonauts on Soviet space stations demonstrated and proved that humans could work and live in space for prolonged periods of time with no lasting harmful effects. The ability to repair, adjust, and install new equipment in space was demonstrated. This success confirmed existing plans to repair satellites and assemble large structures in space.

The Space Shuttle was designed to transport people and cargo between Earth and Earth orbit. The shuttle orbiter was designed for at least 100 missions. The three main engines of the shuttle provide almost a half-million pounds of thrust, which is equivalent to that of the eight engines of Saturn I's first-stage engines. Each engine weighs less than 7,000 pounds but has the power equal to seven Hoover Dams. On April 12, 1981, the first Space Shuttle lifted off. In 1982, it was declared to be an operational vehicle for civilians, military persons, and payloads. The shuttle has opened doors for the eventual possibility of space travel for private citizens.

At the conclusion of the fourth and final test flight of the Space Shuttle on July 4, 1982, President Reagan commented: "The test flights are over, the groundwork has been laid, now we will move forward to capitalize on the tremendous potential offered by the ultimate frontier of space. . . ."

Model Rocketry

Model making is one of the oldest crafts of man. Museums have displays of model boats and other artifacts made by ancient people more than 6,000 years ago. In the twentieth century, the space age has provided the impetus for making model rockets. In the early part of this century, rocket enthusiasts worldwide joined rocket clubs to discuss rocketry and build rockets, an activity that stopped with the advent of World War II. Many of the early model rockets and memorabilia may be found in the National Air and Space Museum of the Smithsonian Institution in Washington, DC.

After the Sputnik launch and the beginning of the space race, there was a resurgence of interest in space sciences. People started experimenting and building their own rockets. Unfortunately, many of these home-made rockets failed. In 1956, the American Rocket Society, since renamed the American Institute of Aeronautics and Astronautics, estimated that one out of seven nonprofessional rocketeers would be killed or hurt while engaged in amateur rocketry.

George Harry Stine, a rocket scientist, was concerned that these tragedies would discourage young people from considering a future in space science. Stine wrote many books, including *Contraband Rockets* (1956) and *Rocket Power and Space Flight* (1957) as well as an article that expressed his concern. Orville Carlisle, an expert pyrotechnic hobbyist, read Stine's article. Understanding the safety problems of model rocketry, Carlisle began to experiment with and design small model rockets. He collaborated with his brother, an avid model airplane hobbyist, and built the first small model rockets in 1954, which sold commercially three years later. This initiated the beginning of the modern era of amateur model rocketry.

Model rocketry today is an extremely safe hobby. Amateur rocketeers no longer need to be concerned about the motors used to propel their rockets. Commercially manufactured motors are not only safe but also easy to use. According to the National Association of Rocketry, in more than 35 million rocket launches, there has not been a serious injury due to motor failure. Rocketeers can now turn their focus to the design of their rockets.

Activities

——— Suggestions for Student Research ———

Many language arts activities, oral and written, can be incorporated into a study of the history of rocketry. The activities can range in difficulty to accommodate students' academic level, depth of understanding, and ability to research the topic.

A student-centered approach to studying rocketry, with a focus on what students want to learn, will motivate students to research. Because many students lack the necessary library skills needed for research, they must learn how to use card catalogs and the various indexes (periodical, social science, newspaper, magazine, etc.) available to them. What the sources are (e.g., encyclopedias, handbooks, audiovisual materials, microforms, newspapers) and how to use them for research are extremely important. Online services should also be considered. Note-taking and outlining skills are necessary to isolate pertinent information for reports, whether oral or written. These techniques help students understand the importance of developing reading comprehension skills.

Research topics might include: the lives of the many rocket scientists involved in rocketry, from its inception to the present day; rocketry and warfare; and an historical time-line, from the Chinese battle of Kai-Keng to today.

Students should be encouraged to include the many advances made by the National Aeronautics and Space Administration. The spin-offs resulting from the program are endless. Suggested topics might include the contributions made to medicine, consumer products, energy and the environment, and public safety.

Students enjoy reading science fiction stories—in particular, the works of Jules Verne and H. G. Wells. Reading these works, as well as other science fiction stories, can stimulate many lively discussions and creative endeavors. Creative writing requires students to use their imagination as well as consider possible future problems for space exploration.

1.1 Balloon Staging

The following activity demonstrates the principle of rocket staging that was first proposed by Johann Schmidlap in the sixteenth century.

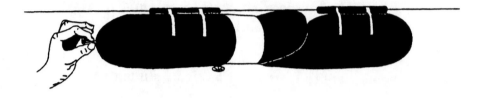

Fig. 1.5. Balloon staging.

Objective

To demonstrate the principle of rocket staging.

Materials

2 long party balloons
Nylon monofilament fishing line
2 plastic straws (milkshake size)
Styrofoam coffee cup
Masking tape
Scissors

Procedure

1. Thread the fishing line through the two straws. Stretch the fishing line taut across a room and secure its ends.

2. Cut the coffee cup in half to create an open-ended ring.

3. Inflate both balloons to stretch them, then release the air. Inflate the first balloon (the second stage) about three-fourths full. Squeeze the open end (nozzle) to keep the air in. Slide the nozzle through the ring. Have another person slide the front end of the second balloon (the first stage) a short distance through the ring as shown in Figure 1.5. Inflate the first-stage balloon. As it inflates, it will press on the nozzle of the second-stage balloon, holding it shut. If this does not work, try inflating the second balloon *before* sliding it in the ring. This step will take practice. Keep holding the nozzle of the inflated first-stage balloon as you proceed and complete step 4.

4. Tape the balloons to the straws (see fig. 1.5). Slide the balloons to the end of the fishing line (in the direction of the balloon nozzles).

5. After a countdown, release the balloon. The escaping gas will propel both balloons along the fishing line. When the first balloon has exhausted its air, it will release the second balloon to continue the trip.

Explanation

In a typical rocket, the stages are mounted one on top of the other, with the lowest stage being the heaviest and largest. When a lower stage has exhausted its load of propellants, the entire stage is dropped. The remaining upper stages have less weight and are more efficient in reaching higher altitudes.

The Space Shuttle has the stages attached side by side. The solid rocket boosters are attached to the side of the external tank. The Shuttle orbiter is also attached to the side of the external tank. When exhausted, the solid rocket boosters are dropped; later, the external tank is dropped.

Chapter Two

Newton's Laws of Motion

Rockets and rocket-powered devices have been in use for more than 2,000 years. However, only during the last 300 years have we discerned the scientific principles behind rocketry. This understanding can be attributed to the English scientist Sir Isaac Newton. In 1687, he published a book titled *Philosophiae Naturalis Principia Mathematica*, commonly referred to as *Principia*. In his writings, Newton explained the three laws of motion that govern all objects on Earth and in space:

1. Objects at rest will stay at rest and objects in motion will stay in motion in a straight line unless acted upon by an unbalanced force.

2. Force is equal to mass times acceleration.

3. For every action there is always an opposite and equal reaction.

The advancement of rocketry, as we know it today, can be attributed to the scientific understanding of Newton's Laws of Motion. First, there must be an unbalanced force (thrust) if a rocket is to lift off from a launch pad. Second, the force produced by a rocket engine depends on the mass of rocket fuel that is burned and how fast the gas escapes the rocket. Third, the motion, or reaction, of the rocket is equal to and in the opposite direction of the action from the engine.

Newton's First Law of Motion

1. *Objects at rest will stay at rest and objects in motion will stay in motion in a straight line unless acted upon by an unbalanced force.*

    To restate Newton's First Law of Motion as it applies to model rocketry: "An unbalanced force must be exerted for a rocket to lift off from a launch pad" (Estes Industries 1985, 65). Students should have an understanding of the terms used in Newton's First Law of Motion as it applies to rocketry.

    Most students are partially aware of the meaning of "at rest." While sitting still on a chair, students are said to be "at rest." However, they are still *moving* because they are sitting on the surface of a spinning planet that is orbiting a star. Although students appear to be at rest, they are actually traveling at a speed of hundreds of kilometers per second. "At rest" is relative because all things are in constant motion at all times; objects at rest are not changing position in relation to the *immediate* surroundings. Hence, when a model rocket is on the launch pad, it is said to be at rest.[1]

    Motion is the opposite of rest. It, too, is relative because all matter in the universe is moving at all times. In Newton's first law, *motion* means that an object "changes position in relation to its surroundings." An example of this can be demonstrated with a ball. It is at rest if it is sitting on the ground, but it is in motion when it is rolling. A model rocket changes its state of rest to one of motion when it leaves the launching pad.

    The term *unbalanced force* is also important. The meaning of this term can be easily demonstrated by holding a ball in your hand and keeping it still. The ball is held in your hand by forces acting upon the ball. The Earth's gravitational force tries to push down the ball while your hand is pushing against the ball to hold it up. The forces are considered to be balanced. If your hand moves or if you let go of the ball, the forces become unbalanced. Students can make a drawing, such as in figure 2.1 on page 17, to demonstrate this principle.

Another example of unbalanced force can easily be demonstrated by having a student sit in a chair. To get up from the chair, the student must exert force. The exertion creates an unbalanced force. Students can think of many other examples demonstrating unbalanced force.

While the rocket is on the launching pad, it is considered to be at rest. The force of gravity pushes the rocket downward while the launching pad pushes against the force of gravity to hold the rocket in position. The model rocket is being acted upon by balanced forces. It is only when the propellant is ignited that the forces becomes unbalanced. The model rocket is then set into motion and will continue in motion in a straight line until another unbalanced force acts upon it.

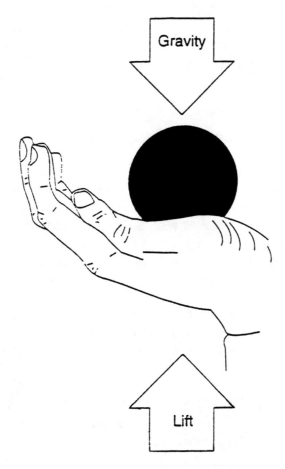

Fig. 2.1. Ball at rest.

To quote the National Aeronautics and Space Administration: "If an object, such as a rocket, is at rest, it takes an unbalanced force to make it move. If the object is already moving, it takes an unbalanced force to stop it, change its direction from a straight line path, or alter its speed" (National Aeronautics and Space Administration 1993, 10).

Newton's Second Law of Motion

2. *Force is equal to mass times acceleration.*

    To restate Newton's Second Law of Motion as it applies to model rocketry: "The amount of thrust (force produced by a rocket engine) will be determined by the mass of rocket fuel that is burned and how fast the gas escapes the rocket. The acceleration of a rocket will be determined by the mass of the rocket and the thrust produced by the engine" (Estes Industries 1985, 65).

    This law can be stated in the formula:

    f = ma

    The letters symbolize the parts of the equation: *f* for force, *m* for mass, and *a* for acceleration. The formula can also be written as:

    a = f/m or **m = f/a**

    However, the first formula, f = ma, is the most commonly used.

    Applying the formula to the launching of model rockets, the mass in the formula (*m*) is the amount of fuel being burned, which in turn expands and escapes from the rocket. Force (*f*) is the thrust that propels the rocket. Acceleration (*a*) is the rate at which the gas escapes. The gas inside the engine of a rocket picks up speed as it leaves the engine; therefore, the greater the mass of the rocket fuel being burned, the faster the gas produced can escape the engine resulting in greater thrust.

    The thrust for a rocket continues as long as the engines are firing. Because the mass is the sum of all its parts, the mass decreases during the flight as the fuel is consumed. The acceleration of the rocket increases as the mass decreases.

    Gifted and middle school students can apply their mathematical skills to determine values for the average acceleration during engine burn (the acceleration phase) based on theoretical "no drag" conditions by using the following formula, which is derived from Newton's Second Law:

$$V_m = (\frac{T}{W_{av}} - 1) gt$$

Vm = average velocity during engine burn

Wav = average weight of rocket (the weight of rocket with engine minus ½ the weight of the propellant)

T = average thrust of rocket engine

g = acceleration due to gravity (32.2 feet/second^2)

t = engine burn time in seconds

The average thrust (*T*) may be calculated using the following formula:

$$T = \frac{\text{total impulse}}{\text{burn time}}$$

The necessary values may be obtained and/or calculated from the information included in most model rocket manufacturers' catalogs.

In the metric system, weight is a unit of force called the Newton (N). Because f = ma, the weight in Newtons equals mass (in kilograms) times the acceleration of gravity (9.81 m/s^2).

The Newton car (see fig. 2.2) demonstrates Newton's Second Law of Motion.

Newton's Third Law of Motion

3. *For every action there is an opposite and equal reaction.*

To restate Newton's Third Law of Motion as it applies to model rocketry: "The reaction, or motion, of the rocket is equal to and in an opposite direction from the action, or escaping gas, from the engine" (Estes Industries 1985, 65).

To demonstrate the Third Law of Motion, the teacher can make a working model of a Hero engine (see fig. 2.3, page 23). The activity is not intended for children; it is primarily intended for instructor use as a demonstration tool.

Note

1. Advanced students may want to research Einstein's Theory of Relativity as it relates to motion. Einstein's classic train example demonstrated relativity simply: Imagine a train with passenger cars traveling along a track. A child on the train tosses a ball into the air and catches it. To an observer on the train, the ball rises straight up in the air and back down again. To a stationary observer outside the train, the ball rises and falls in an arc along the track.

References

Estes Industries. 1985. *Estes Manual.* Penrose, CO: Estes Industries.

National Aeronautics and Space Administration. 1993. *Rockets.* Washington, D.C.: NASA.

Activities

2.1 Newton Car

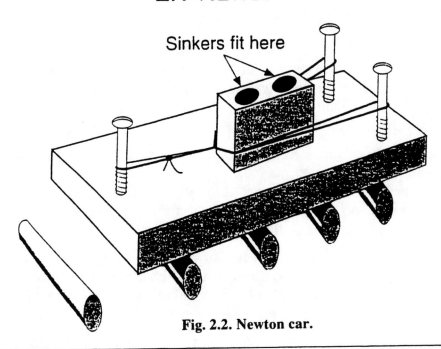

Sinkers fit here

Fig. 2.2. Newton car.

Objective

To demonstrate Newton's Second Law of Motion by showing the reaction of a rolling car by increasing its mass and acceleration.

Materials

Wooden block, approximately 10 x 20 x 2.5 cm

Wooden block, approximately 7.5 x 5 x 2.5 cm

3 three-inch No. 10 wood screws (round head)

12 round pencils or short lengths of similar dowel rods

3 rubber bands

Cotton string

Matches

6 lead fishing sinkers, approximately ½ ounce each

Drill and bit (bit size determined by the diameter of the fishing sinkers)

Vice

Screwdriver

Meter stick

Procedure

1. Screw the three screws into the large wooden block as shown in figure 2.2.

2. Hold the short piece of wood with a vice and drill two holes, each large enough to hold two sinkers.

3. Tie the string into several small loops of the same size.

4. Place one string loop over a rubber band and then place the ends of the rubber band over the two screws on one end of the large wood block. Pull the rubber band back like a slingshot and slip the string over the third screw to hold the rubber band taut.

5. On a level table top, arrange the pencils or dowel rods in a row, like railroad ties. Be sure to mark the position of each dowel rod to ensure the integrity of this experiment through repeated trials. Place the large block on one end of the row so that the tip of each screw points toward a dowel rod. Slip the small block without sinkers into the rubber bands.

6. Light a match and ignite the ends of the string hanging down from the loop. When the string burns through, the rubber band will throw the block off the car and the car will roll in the other direction. Measure how far the car travels along the table top.

7. Reset the equipment and add a second rubber band. Again, light the string, then measure how far the car travels along the table top.

8. Reset the equipment and try again with three rubber bands. Then try again with one rubber band and two sinkers, four sinkers, and so on.

9. Plot the data from each of the experiments on a graph.

Explanation

In this activity, students are able to test a slingshot-like device that throws a wooden block, causing the car to move in the opposite direction. Through repeated trials of this experiment, it will become clear that the distance the car travels depends on the number of rubber bands used and the mass of the block being ejected. The mass of the block can be increased by adding sinkers to the block. Many opportunities to combine science and math are possible with this activity.

2.2 Hero Engine

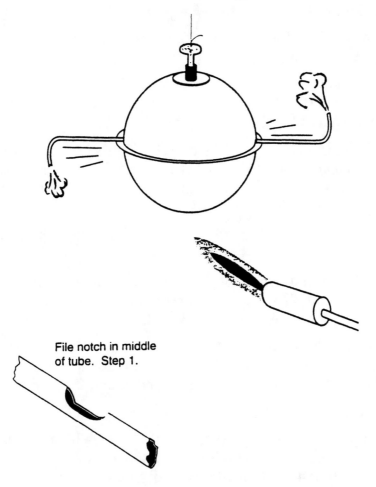

File notch in middle
of tube. Step 1.

Fig. 2.3. Hero engine.

Objective

To demonstrate Newton's Third Law of Motion using an action force of expanding steam or falling water.

Materials

Copper toilet tank float (available from full-line hardware stores)

Thumb screw, $\frac{1}{4}$-inch diameter

Brass tube, 12-inch length, $\frac{3}{16}$-inch inside diameter (available from hobby shops)

Solder

Fishing line

Ice pick or drill

Metal file

Propane torch

Procedure

Making a Steam-Powered Hero Engine

1. File the middle of the brass tube until a notch is produced (see fig. 2.3). Do not file the tube in half.

2. Using the ice pick or drill, bore two small holes on opposite sides of the float at its middle. The holes should be just large enough to pass the tube straight through the float.

3. With the tube positioned so that equal lengths protrude through the float, heat the contact points of the float and tube with the propane torch. Touch the end of the solder to the heated area so that it melts and seals both joints.

4. Drill a water access hole through the threaded connector at the top of the float.

5. Using the torch again, heat the protruding tubes approximately 2.5 cm from each end. With pliers, carefully bend the tube tips in opposite directions. Bend the tubes slowly so they do not crimp.

6. Drill a small hole through the flat part of the thumb screw for attaching the fish line and swivel. Twist the thumb screw into the threaded connector of the float, as in step 4, and attach the line and swivel.

Using a Steam-Powered Hero Engine

1. Place a small amount of water into the float. The precise amount is not important. The float can be filled through the top, if you drilled an access hole, or through the tubes by partially immersing the engine in a bowl of water with one tube submerged and the other out of the water.

2. Suspend the engine and heat its bottom with the torch. The engine should begin spinning within two minutes. Be careful not to operate the engine too long because it probably will not be exactly balanced and may wobble violently. If it begins to wobble, remove the heat.

2.3 Rocket Pinwheel

Using air instead of steam, students make a rocket pinwheel that uses the action-reaction principle to make the pinwheel move.

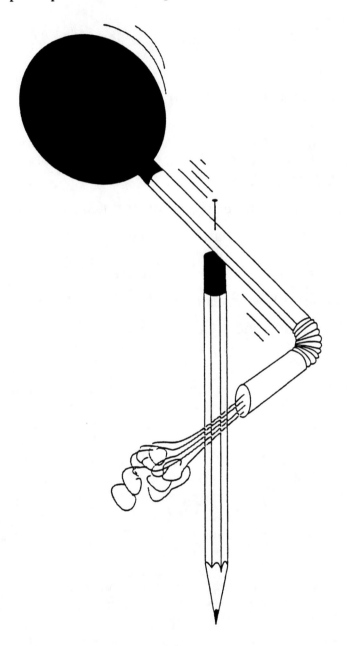

Fig. 2.4. Rocket pinwheel.

Objective

To demonstrate Newton's Third Law of Motion using escaping air from a balloon as the action force.

Materials

Wooden pencil with an eraser

Straight pin

Round balloon

Flexible soda straw

Procedure

1. Inflate the balloon to stretch it out.

2. Slip the nozzle end of the balloon over the end of the straw farthest away from the flexible bend. Use a short piece of plastic tape to seal the balloon to the straw. The balloon should inflate when you blow through the straw.

3. Bend the opposite end of the straw at a right angle (see fig. 2.4).

4. Lay the straw and the balloon on an outstretched finger to find the balance point. Push the pin through the straw at the balance point into the pencil eraser and into the wood itself.

5. Spin the straw a few times to enlarge the pinhole.

6. Inflate the balloon and let go of the straw.

Explanation

The air escaping from the straw is the action force, which causes a reaction: The straw and balloon rotate together in the opposite direction of the action.

Some toy and variety stores sell an inexpensive balloon-powered helicopter. The device has three small plastic wings through which air passes and is released in a right-angle direction at each blade tip. One of these toys is marketed under the name of Whistle Balloon Helicopter, which was used by astronauts on the STS-54 Space Shuttle mission during the Physics of Toys live lesson.

Students will reinforce their understanding of Newton's Third Law of Motion by relating the law to their own experiences. As an example, they can better understand the concept as it applies to skateboarding. When a person jumps off the skateboard, the skateboard moves in the opposite direction. Jumping off is the action and the skateboard moving in the opposite direction is the reaction (see fig. 2.5).

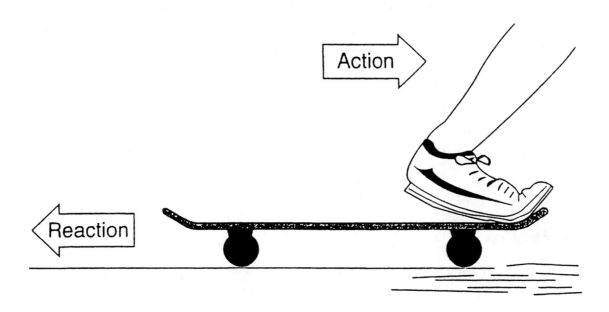

Fig. 2.5. Skateboard and the Third Law of Motion.

When the distance traveled by the rider and the skateboard are compared, it may appear that the skateboard had a much greater reaction. However, the reason the skateboard traveled farther is that it had less mass than the rider.

The movement of the air surrounding the rider and the skateboard slows down the action. This movement through the air causes friction, or "drag." Drag impedes the action-reaction. In space, where there is no air, less of the rocket's energy is consumed to overcome friction. While on the ground, the escaping gas from a rocket has to push against the air. This, in turn, uses up some of the energy of the rocket. Where there is no air, as in space, the gases can escape freely. It is the surrounding air that impedes the action-reaction.

2.4 A Balloon and Air Pressure

A simple activity using a toy balloon lets students observe the action-reaction principle in Newton's Third Law of Motion.

Objective

To demonstrate Newton's Third Law of Motion.

Materials

Balloon

Procedure

1. Fill the balloon with air. Hold the opening of the balloon tightly shut to prevent the air from escaping.

2. Release the opening to let the air escape.

Explanation

When the balloon is filled with air and there is no opening, the air inside the balloon is compressed and exerts a uniform pressure inside the balloon in all directions. When the compressed air is released through the small opening used to fill the balloon, it will shoot across the room. The higher the pressure of the air rushing out causes the balloon to fly off in the opposite direction.

In a rocket, propellants are burned to develop gas pressure similar to the simple balloon experiment. The gas rushing out from the rocket propels it on its flight. For the rocket to leave the launching pad, the thrust from the engine has to be greater than the mass of the rocket. It is the action of the expelling gas that propels the rocket in the opposite direction, which is the reaction.

2.5 Rocket Car

Students can construct a balloon-powered rocket car that will roll across the floor when air is forced to escape through a plastic straw.

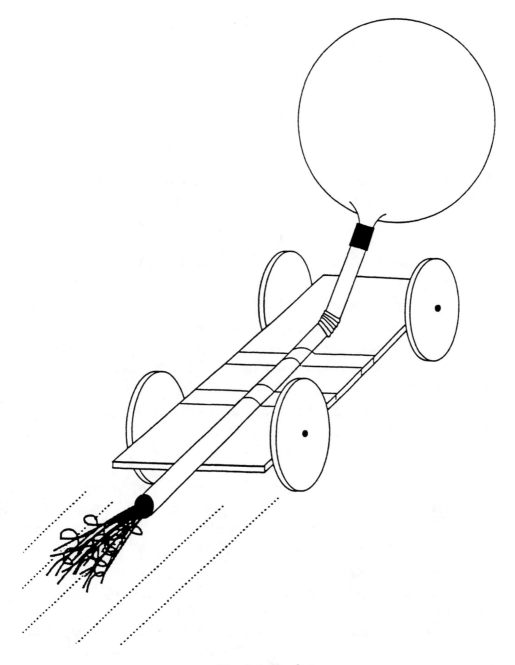

Fig. 2.6. Rocket car.

Objective

To demonstrate Newton's Third Law of Motion with escaping air as the action force.

Materials

4 pins
Styrofoam meat tray
Cellophane tape
Flexi-straw
Scissors
Drawing compass
Marking pen
Small balloon
Ruler

Procedure

1. Using the ruler, marking pen, and drawing compass, draw a 7.5-by-18-cm rectangle and four 7.5-cm-diameter circles on the flat surface of the meat tray. Cut out each piece.

2. Inflate the balloon a few times to stretch it. Slip the nozzle over the end of the flexi-straw with tape and seal it tight so that the balloon can be inflated by blowing through the straw.

3. Tape the straw to the car, as shown in fig. 2.6.

4. Push one pin into the center of each circle and then into the edge of the rectangle, as shown. The pins become axles for the wheels. Do not push the pins in snugly because the wheels have to rotate freely. It is okay if the wheels wobble.

5. Inflate the balloon and pinch the straw to hold in the air. Set the car on a smooth surface and release the straw.

Explanation

The escaping air is the action and the movement of the car in the opposite direction is the reaction. The car's wheels reduce the friction and provide some stability to the car's motion. A well-designed and well-constructed car will travel several meters in a straight line across a smooth floor.

Students can design other cars of varying sizes. The bottoms of Styrofoam cups can be cut off and used as wheels. With their cars, students can hold distance trials on the floor. They can measure the distance covered and graph the distance that each car travels. Averaging the multiple runs gives students additional math activities.

Chapter Three

Basic Parts of a Model Rocket

As students become more skilled in making model rockets or using more advanced commercial kits, they will possibly be designing and constructing their own rockets. The beginning rocketeer, however, should use a factory-built model rocket kit, because these rockets have already been tested for safety and stability by the manufacturer. When having students construct their rockets, it is essential that the teacher and students know the names of the parts of the rocket, as shown in figure 3.1.

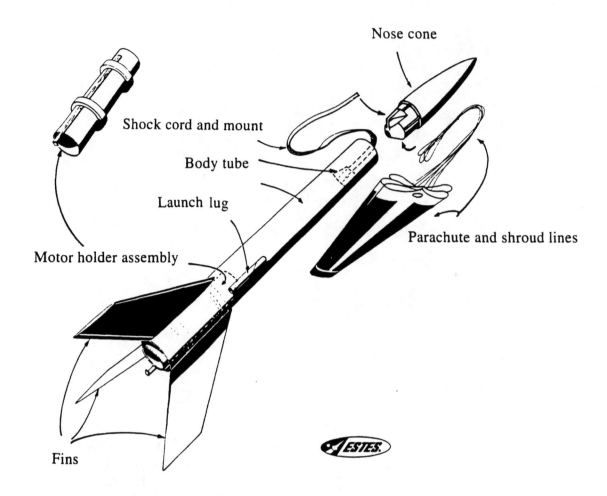

Fig. 3.1. Parts of a model rocket. Used with permission of Estes Industries.

The following information and brief description of the various parts of a beginning model rocket will aid in understanding the function of those parts.

Recovery System

A recovery system provides a way to resist the force of gravity and prevents the rocket from falling too rapidly to the ground due to the force of gravity. There are six types of recovery systems: featherweight, tumble, streamer, helicopter, glide, and parachute. Generally, the parachute recovery system is used for beginning rocketeers.

Most children enjoy hearing about the first parachute. Leonardo da Vinci (1452–1519) is considered the inventor of the parachute. He called his parachute a "tent of linen." His parachute was pyramid shaped, with a pole extending from the apex to the point where the shroud lines met (see fig. 3.2).

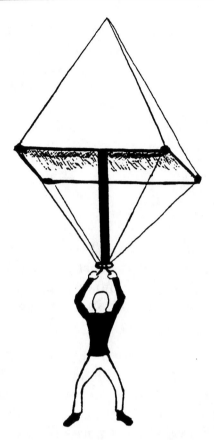

Fig. 3.2. Leonardo da Vinci's parachute.

He based his parachute on the scientific principle that an object offers as much resistance to the air as the air does to the object. In Leonardo da Vinci's words, "The movement of the air against a fixed thing is as great as the movement of the movable thing against the air which is immovable" (Heydenrich 1951, 14). Some scholars believe that he successfully tested his parachute from a tower that he had built for that purpose.

Some form of recovery system (e.g., a parachute) is necessary to slow the rocket's fall and to prevent damage when it lands. The rising air fills the parachute and slows its descent. In a vacuum, a parachute would fall without any resistance. Unlike a vacuum, air in the atmosphere has mass and resists gravity's pull, which slows the descent of the parachute. The speed of the descending parachute is directly proportionate to the mass of the air. For example, in humid air, the parachute would fall slower than in drier air, because the water vapor increases the air's mass. In addition, the broader the area of the canopy of the parachute, the more resistance created by the air and the slower the parachute falls.

Students like to design their own parachutes, whether triangular, square, pentagonal, or hexagonal (a lesson on geometric shapes can accompany this activity). To prevent student-made parachutes from crashing to the ground with their rockets, it is best to let students test their parachutes by hand-tossing them with weights attached. By timing the descent of their handmade parachutes, students can evaluate the efficiency of their designs. They can also test the suitability of various materials for parachutes.

Fins

The chief function of the fins is to guide and stabilize the flight of the rocket. The aerodynamic surface created by the fins on a rocket gives directional stability. For a model rocket to reach its maximum altitude, the fins must have a smooth surface, achieved by sanding, sealing, and painting.

The placement and size of the fins are critical to achieving adequate stability without adding too much weight. The activities in this chapter provide students with the opportunity to construct small paper rockets and test them with and without fins. Students will soon discover that a rocket without fins is much more difficult to control.

Launching System

The launching platform provides a stable base for the model rocket. It is essential that the launch pad rest on firm ground. The launch lug on the side of the rocket guides the rocket during the first few feet of flight until it leaves the launch rod. The exhaust gas from the rocket is deflected by the blast deflector.

The model rocket's solid propellant motor is loaded into the motor mount. *Only commercially manufactured motors should be used!* The motor is placed inside the holder tube, which has been glued inside the model rocket. Follow the directions for the assembly of the motor holder tube carefully. There are various motor types used in model rockets, ranging from small motors to very large ones. At school, the smaller motors should be used by beginning model rocketeers.

The ignition system is electrical and ignites the combustion process in the rocket motor. An electric current coming through the wires from the launch controller heats up the propellant inside the rocket, causing the propellant to burn. A commercial launch controller is available that makes launching rockets safe and easy. It has a safety key that must be in the launch controller before the electric current can be activated. The safety key must *never* be in the launch controller when someone is placing a rocket on the launch rod or attaching the microchips to the propellant. Only after everyone is 15 feet away from the launch pad should the safety key be inserted into the launch controller. In a classroom it is easy to misplace a safety key, so it is always wise to have spare safety keys available to avoid a possible disappointment for the students prior to launching.

References

Heydenrich, Ludwig Heinrich. 1951. *Leonardo da Vinci the Scientist.* New York: International Business.

Activities

3.1 Making a Parachute

Objective

To understand the effect of air resistance and gravity on a parachute.

Materials

White cloth (a variety of fabrics should be available to students)
64-inch length of string
Magic markers
Washers
Scissors
Yardsticks and rulers
Hole puncher

Procedure

1. Cut the cloth into 1-square-foot pieces.

2. Punch a small hole $\frac{1}{2}$ inch from each corner.

3. Have students draw designs on the cloth to personalize their chutes.

4. Measure the string into four 16-inch segments and cut.

5. Tie the string segments into each of the holes in the four corners of the cloth.

7. Gather the four strings together and tie the ends to the washer.

8. Wrap the strings and washer around the cloth parachute.

Testing the Parachutes

Have students test their parachutes outside. To further investigate the effect air resistance has on parachutes, have students make parachutes with and without holes to test the effect on air resistance. When making their parachutes, students should take great care to avoid puncturing a hole, regardless of how small, in the parachute.

Explanation

Shroud lines are attached to the parachute and the nose of the rocket. The force of the motor's ejection charge deploys the parachute, which is attached to the shock cord. In Estes's Alpha rocket, a beginner's model, the shock cord is a strong elastic cord attached to the inside of the rocket and the parachute. Follow the directions carefully for mounting the shock cord.

Recovery wadding, tissue that has been treated with a fire retardant, is placed inside the rocket tube prior to launching. The wadding is packed between the model rocket motor and the parachute to protect the parachute from the ejection gases. Discuss the need for flame-resistant wadding and demonstrate to the class how the wadding does not burn. The importance of having flame-resistant wadding cannot be overstressed.

3.2 Paper Rocket

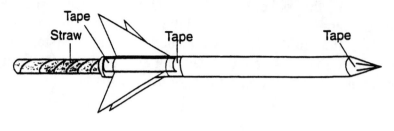

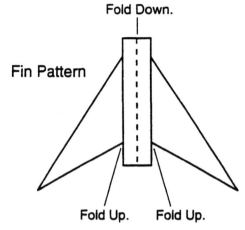

Fig. 3.3. Paper rocket.

Objective

To demonstrate the importance of using control systems, such as fins, to stabilize rockets in flight.

Materials

Scrap bond paper

Cellophane tape

Scissors

Sharpened fat pencil

Milkshake straw (slightly thinner than a pencil)

Procedure

1. Cut a narrow rectangular strip of paper about 13 centimeters long and roll it tightly around the fat pencil. Tape the cylinder and remove it from the pencil.

2. Cut points into one end of the cylinder to make a cone and slip it back onto the pencil.

3. Slide the cone end onto the pencil tip. Squeeze and tape it together to seal the end and form a nose cone. The pencil point provides support for

taping. An alternative method is to fold one end of the tape over the tip and seal it with tape around the bottom edge.

4. Remove the cylinder from the pencil and gently blow into the open end to check for leaks. If air escapes, use more tape to seal the leaks.

5. Cut out two sets of fins using the pattern shown in figure 3.3. Fold according to instructions. Tape the fins near the open end of the cylinder. The tabs make taping easy.

6. Slip the straw into the rocket's opening and point the rocket in a safe direction. To avoid any possible eye injury it is important that the rocket not be aimed toward anyone.

7. Blow sharply through the straw.

Explanation

Students can test their paper rockets by varying the placement of the fins on the rocket. By making different sizes of fins they can measure the distances traveled in order to determine what makes one rocket perform better than the other. Each student can plot his or her own results as well as average the results of all students.

3.3 Pencil Rocket

The following pencil rocket activity is intended for middle school students.

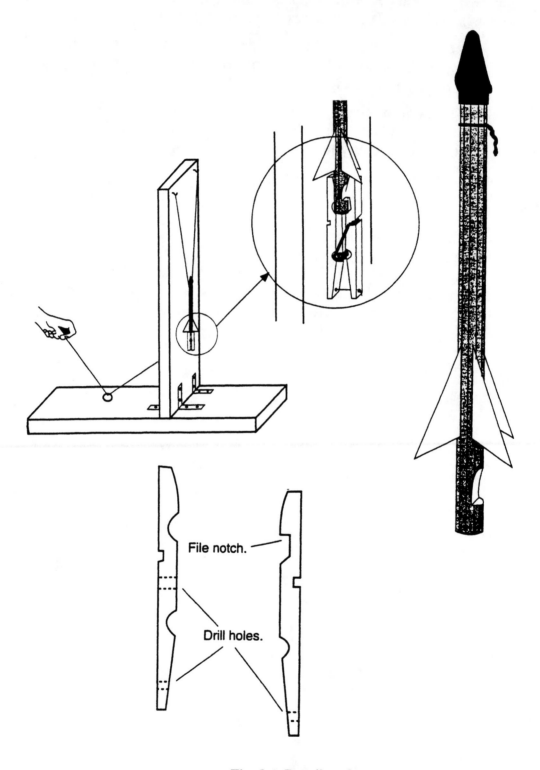

File notch.

Drill holes.

Fig. 3.4. Pencil rocket.

Objective

To demonstrate the effect fins have on rocket flight through the atmosphere.

Materials

2 pieces of wood about 1 meter by 7.5 centimeters (thickness can vary)

2 cup hooks

Wooden spring clothespin

Small wood screw

Screw eye

4 metal angle irons and screws

4 feet of heavy string

Iron baling wire

Several rubber bands

Several unsharpened wooden pencils

Several pencil cap erasers

Cellophane or masking tape

Heavy paper

Saw

Wood file

Drill and $\frac{3}{16}$-inch bit

Pliers

Procedure

Making a Launch Platform

1. Join the two pieces of wood to form the launch platform (see fig. 3.4). Use metal angle irons on each side to strengthen the structure.

2. Screw the cup hooks and screw eye into the wood, as shown in figure 3.4.

3. Disassemble the clothespin and file the jaw of one wood piece square, as shown in figure 3.4.

4. Drill a hole through the upright piece of the launch platform and screw the clothespin to the upright piece so that the lower holes in the clothespin line up with the hole in the upright board. Reassemble the clothespin.

5. Tie a big knot in one end of the string and feed it through the clothespin, through the upright piece of the platform, and then through the screw eye. When the free end of the string is pulled, the string will not slip out of the hole, and the clothespin will open. The clothespin has become a rocket hold-and-release device.

6. Loop four rubber bands together and loop their ends onto the cup hooks. The launch platform is now complete.

Making the Rocket

1. Take a short piece of baling wire and wrap it around the eraser end of the pencil about 2.5 centimeters from the end. Use pliers to twist the wire tightly so that it "bites" into the wood a bit. Next, bend the twisted ends into a hook.

2. Take a sharp knife and cut a notch into the other end of the pencil.

3. Cut out small paper rocket fins and tape them to the pencil just above the notch.

4. Place an eraser cap over the upper end of the rocket end. This blunts the nose to make the rocket safer if it hits something.

Launching the Rocket

1. Choose an open area in which to launch the rocket.

2. Spread open the jaw of the clothespin and place the notched end of the rocket in the jaws. Close the jaws and gently pull the pencil upward to ensure that the rocket is secure. If the rocket does not fit, change the shape of the notch slightly.

3. Pull the rubber bands down and loop them over the wire hook. **Caution:** Be sure not to look down over the rocket as you do this, in case the rocket is released prematurely.

4. Stand at the other end of the launcher and step on the wood to provide additional support.

5. You, as the teacher, should stand next to the launch pad and make sure no one, except you, is standing next to the launch pad. Count down from 5 and pull the string. Step away from the rocket as it flies (about 20 meters high, after which it will turn upside down and return to the ground).

6. The rocket's terminal altitude can be adjusted by increasing or decreasing the tension on the rubber bands.

Explanation

In this activity, students can fly pencil rockets using a rubber-band-powered launch gantry. Like Robert Goddard's first liquid-fuel rocket in 1926, the pencil rocket gets its upward thrust from the nose area rather than the tail. Regardless, the rocket's fins still provide the stability and guide the rocket upward for a smooth flight. If a steady wind is blowing during flight, the fins will steer the rocket toward the wind in a process that is referred to as "weather cocking." Active controls steer NASA rockets during flight to prevent weather cocking and to aim them on the right trajectory. Active controls include tilting nozzles and various forms of fins and vanes.

Chapter Four

Making the Model Rocket

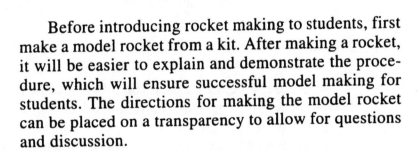

Before introducing rocket making to students, first make a model rocket from a kit. After making a rocket, it will be easier to explain and demonstrate the procedure, which will ensure successful model making for students. The directions for making the model rocket can be placed on a transparency to allow for questions and discussion.

Beginning Construction

Before starting rocket making, have each student bring an empty shoe box to school for his or her model rocket kit. The shoe box provides a place for the student to keep his or her rocket and prevents the loss of the small parts. It also prevents any disagreement as to whose rocket is whose.

Besides a rocket kit for each student, have these additional materials needed to make the rocket:

rulers

pencils

scissors

white glue

sandpaper

sanding sealer

spray paint in various colors

masking tape

decals

The time needed to finish the rockets depends on many factors. Although the rockets can be finished in a week, it is best to allow more time because of student absences, school functions, and the amount of time taken to add the finishing touches to the rockets. At times, a student may break a fin or incorrectly glue the motor mount tube in the body of the rocket. Extra parts will then be needed. After construction has started, you can usually gauge the time needed to finish the rockets. I generally allow three weeks for construction due to the possibility of construction mishaps.

Painting the Models

Here is an easy method for spray painting the model rockets. Besides the spray paint, all you need are old newspapers, masking tape, a large cardboard box, and one metal coat hanger for each student. Instead of completing the rocket before spraying, I have found it best to have only the fins and launch lug (prepared as per the manufacturer's directions) glued to the body tube of the rocket prior to spraying it. The nose cone, without the shock cord and parachute attached, can be placed on the body tube for spray painting if the student wants to paint it as well. If desired, the nose cone can be painted later.

One student's desk or a table should be taken outside and covered with newspaper before the cardboard box is placed on the desk. The paper should be taped to the desk to prevent movement. Next, students should bend their metal coat hangers so that a small part of the hanger will fit inside the body tube. The hook end should be outside of the rocket for the student to hold while painting the rocket. In this way, the student can hold the rocket away from himself or herself and avoid inhaling paint fumes. Have students hold their rockets inside the box while painting them. Rotating the rocket quickly, much like a barbecue spit, will allow for an even coat of paint.

A long piece of string can be used, much like a clothesline, in the classroom, to allow the painted rockets to dry evenly and completely. The rocket can be hung by the hook of the hanger. To prevent quarrels over which rocket belongs to which student, have students tape name tags on the coat hangers.

Hanging up rockets to dry.

While rockets are drying, students can assemble other parts. Follow the manufacturer's directions carefully when completing the model rocket.

Finishing Touches

Students always enjoy personalizing their rockets. Provide different colored paints and decals so students can create custom designs.

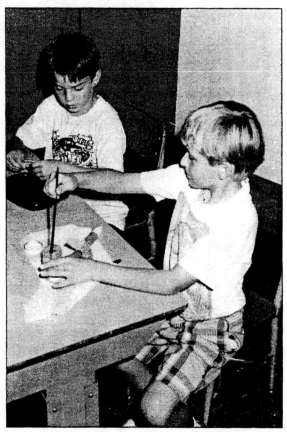

Sealing fins and applying decals.

While some students prefer having a single color of paint for their rockets, others may want to have several colors on their rockets. To achieve this effect, use masking tape to cover portions of the rocket. Then the student can spray the uncovered portions. When the painted part of the rocket is *completely* dry, remove the masking tape. Then mask the painted part of the rocket, and spray it with an additional color.

There are many enamel paints that can be used on model rockets. The brush-on enamels are easy to work with, dry quickly, and usually require only one coat. If brush-on enamels are used, you will need a high-quality brush to avoid brush marks.

It is easier to paint a rocket a solid color and then use the decals provided with the rocket kit to personalize it than to paint a rocket with two or more colors. The decals are easy to apply. If desired, you can purchase decals with different designs at any hobby store. It is a good idea to always have extra decals available as students sometimes tear them when they are applying them. After the decals are completely dry, a coat of clear spray paint can be used to protect them. Hair spray can also be used, but it is not as satisfactory as clear spray paint.

During the construction phase and after the rocket is completely finished, students usually want to take their rockets home before the launch. This should never be allowed. To do so is to invite trouble. Rockets will come back broken or changed so that they are no longer safe. Let the students know that after the launch is over they can take their rockets home but not before.

Chapter Five

Preparing for Lift Off

Materials Needed for the Launch

Getting started with rockets can be as exciting for the teacher or parent as it is for the student. There are many different starter kits on the market that provide everything needed. It is generally less expensive to purchase a kit that includes the launch controller and launch pad than it is to purchase these elements separately. If a starter kit is purchased, you must buy additional rockets, wadding, batteries, and igniters for the rest of the class. Everything needed for a rocket launch can be purchased separately, if desired. Many hobby stores offer discounts for teachers.

An excellent beginning rocket is the Alpha skill-level 1 rocket manufactured by Estes Industries. The rocket kit is complete, the directions are easy to follow, and the rocket is simple to make. The only extra material needed to make this rocket is white glue, scissors, sandpaper, sanding sealer, and rulers.

Wadding is essential for all launches. The flame-retardant wadding will prevent the parachute or rocket from being burned. At no time should any other paper or material be used when packing a rocket for flight. Packages of wadding can be purchased at hobby stores.

A launch pad is necessary for any launch. It is a permanent acquisition that can be used repeatedly. The launch pad includes a blast deflector that prevents the motor exhaust from hitting the ground and possibly causing a fire. A launch rod, which provides stability for the rocket, is also included with the pad. The rod guides the rocket as it picks up speed during its first few feet of flight. A rocket must be launched from the launch pad with a launch rod. *Never launch a rocket by just setting the rocket on its fins on the ground.*

There are many different sizes of model rocket motors, also referred to as engines. (An engine has moving parts but a motor turns chemical energy into mechanical energy so the term motor is used in this book.) In a starter kit, the right motor for the specific rocket is already included. The motors are classified from $\frac{1}{4}$ A, which has the least power, up to 0, which is the most powerful motor. Beginning rocketeers should start with motor A, which gives tremendous thrust but keeps the rocket from ascending so high that it will be lost. Take into account that the higher the rocket travels, the less chance there will be for recovery of the rocket. Many schools place limitations on the type of motor that can be used so check with your school's safety code first.

Model rocket motors are always ignited electrically using special igniters. A match or fuse is *never* used. Model rocket igniters work on the same principle as an electric stove or toaster. The resistance of the igniter's wire causes electrical energy flowing through it to be transformed into heat. When the wire gets hot, a chemical initiator on the end of the igniter burns, igniting the motor's propellant. Commercially manufactured electrical launch systems, such as Estes Industries's Solar Launch Controller, are designed for safety and provide all the power needed to launch a model rocket.

Because every rocket flight uses up the igniter and the motor, it is necessary to have extra igniters and motors. Extra batteries for the launch controller are needed for back up. Temporary repair materials, such as masking, cellophane, or duct tape, should be at the launch site. At times, a burned-out motor is difficult to remove. Needle-nose pliers will usually do the job. It may be necessary to replace burned-out batteries in the controller; some types of controllers may require the use of a screwdriver.

Although not essential for launching rockets, other materials can make the experience more enjoyable. Students like using a stop watch and an altitude tracking device at the launch site. Writing materials, such as paper, pencils, and clipboards, should be available for both the timing and tracking operators. Binoculars help students trace the flight of their rockets. Having a camera ready for the action makes the launch more memorable as everyone enjoys having pictures taken of the launch. These pictures will provide students with a lasting memory of their launch.

Selecting a Site and Obtaining Necessary Approval

Selecting the proper site for launching is critical. The site should be away from trees, power lines, and buildings. The recovery area needs to be at least one-fourth the maximum height the rocket will reach. (The rocket's maximum altitude depends on the size of the motor.) The launch pad should be placed in the center of the launch and recovery area.

Once the launch site is selected, get the approval of the school principal. Next, notify the fire department and tell them when and where the launch is going to be held. The fire department will come to the location to check on the safety of the launch site. After receiving approval from the fire department, file a letter of request for the launching activity with the safety department of the school district. The school district's safety department gives the final written approval for launching rockets on school premises.

The parents of students who will be launching rockets should be notified. Include a brief statement about the safety of the launch as well as the other rocket activities planned and request written approval from the parents, which will involve them in the rocket launch. Almost all parents want their child to participate and parents look forward to attending the launch.

Pre-Launch Checklist

Use the pre-launch checklist (fig. 5.1) to organize your preparations. Follow the items in the order listed for a trouble-free launch.

Pre-Launch Checklist

Class _____

Launch Date _____

Launch Time _____

Launch Site _____

☐ Select the launch and recovery site

☐ Get the principal's approval of launch date and time

☐ Get and post the fire department's approval

☐ Get the district's safety department's written approval

☐ Get the administrator's approval of launching date and time

☐ Notify teachers and parents of assembly date, time, and location

☐ Notify teachers and parents of launch date, time, and location

☐ Arrange for the school's media specialist or local newspaper reporters and TV stations to be at the launch

☐ Review safety codes with students

☐ Measure and show students the distance they will be from the launching pad (Distance depends on the size of the motor.)

☐ Complete sample rocket for demonstration

☐ Launch sample rocket for demonstration

☐ Have students prepare rockets: pack rockets with parachutes and wadding; insert motors in motor mounts

☐ Secure igniters to preclude unauthorized launching by students

☐ Write numbers on rocket storage boxes in the order in which rockets will be launched

Fig. 5.1. Pre-launch checklist.

Safety Activities

The importance of stressing safety to students cannot be overemphasized. Discuss each item of the safety code (fig. 5.2, page 55). The National Association of Rocketry (NAR) was formed in 1957 to promote national competitions and to develop standards and safety codes for model rocketry. Estes Industries, which makes different types of model rockets, followed the NAR-established safety codes to write safety codes for children.

A myriad of activities embracing language arts, math, and science can reinforce an understanding of the safety code. As class discussions are held, there will be areas that need more clarification and new ideas will materialize as a result of these discussions.

One item of the safety code, number 14, involves pre-launch research activities. This activity is only intended for older students. Elementary school students should use factory-made rocket kits, but you should still discuss this code with the younger students.

Launching a rocket without a recovery system allows students to observe what happens to the rocket. It may fall to the ground so quickly that the rocket breaks and can't be launched until it is properly repaired. The model rocket might land on an overhead power line at which time it is left where it landed. Tell the students why the rocket has to stay there until the power company gets it down.

Checking the manufacturers' recommendations for weight limits, students can weigh their rockets to compare the recommended weight with the actual weight of their model rockets. Students can make a graph showing this comparison as well as a comparison of the manufacturers' assumed rocket altitudes with their rockets' actual altitudes.

Although manufacturers' model rockets have already been checked for stability, older students should be taught about the stability of model rockets. Regardless of the size, shape, or mass of a model rocket, there is a point called the *center of mass* (CM), where the rocket is balanced perfectly. One can demonstrate this point by balancing an object, like a ruler, on a finger. The CM is usually at the halfway point on the ruler. By taping a nail or other object on one end of the ruler, students can observe how the center of mass changes to a point closer to the object. (Older students can research the effect of the *center of pressure* on model rockets and write research reports. For the younger students, finding the center of mass is sufficient.)

A simple way for younger students to check the stability of a rocket is to find the place where their rocket is balanced. Have the students tie a long string around the rocket at this point, swing their rocket, and observe what happens. Because manufacturers pretest the stability of model rockets, students' rockets will be stable. To demonstrate instability, have students make several demonstration rockets without fins or with misaligned fins. When students swing these rockets, they will notice the differences in "flight" patterns.

Making posters, bulletin boards, and collages depicting the principles of safety is another way of reviewing the safety codes. After completion of their art project, students can give oral reports explaining which safety codes were depicted in the art work.

Students can devise tests about rocketry safety. They enjoy making up their own tests, and this, in itself, serves as an additional reinforcement.

Model Rocketry Safety Code

1. *Construction*—My model rocket will be made of lightweight materials such as paper, wood, plastic, and rubber, without any metal as structural parts.

2. *Engines*—I will use only pre-loaded, factory-made NAR Safety Certified model rocket engines in the manner recommended by the manufacturer. I will not alter these engines in any way nor attempt to reload these engines.

3. *Recovery*—I will always use a recovery system that will return my rockets safely to the ground so that they may be flown again.

4. *Weight Limits*—My model rocket will weigh no more than 453 grams (16 oz.) at lift-off and the engine will contain no more than 113 grams (4 oz.) of propellant.

5. *Stability*—I will check the stability of my rocket before its first flight, except when launching models with certified stability.

6. *Launching System*—The system I use to launch my model rockets will be remotely controlled and electrically operated, and will contain a switch that returns to the "off" position when released. I will remain at least 15 feet from any rocket that is being launched.

7. *Launch Safety*—I will not let anyone approach a model rocket on a launcher until I have made sure that either the safety interlock key has been removed or the battery has been disconnected from my launcher.

8. *Flying Conditions*—I will not launch my model rockets in high winds; near buildings, power lines, tall trees, or low-flying aircraft; or under any conditions that might be dangerous to people or property.

9. *Launch Area*—My model rockets will always be launched from a cleared area, free of any flammable materials, and I will only use flame-resistant recovery wadding in my rockets.

10. *Jet Deflector*—My launcher will have a jet deflector device to prevent the engine exhaust from contacting the ground directly.

11. *Launch Rod*—To prevent accidental eye injury, I will always place the launcher so that the end of the rod is above eye level or cap the end of the rod with my hand when approaching it. I will never place my head or body over the launching rod. When my launcher is not in use I will always store it so that the launch rod is not in an upright position.

(Safety Code continues.)

From *Blast Off!* © 1997. Teacher Ideas Press. (800) 237-6124.

Model Rocketry Safety Code (Cont.)

12. *Power Lines*—I will never attempt to recover my rocket from power lines or other dangerous places.

13. *Launch Targets and Angles*—I will not launch rockets so that their flight path will carry them against targets on the ground, and will never use an explosive warhead nor a payload that is intended to be flammable. My launching device will always be pointed within 30 degrees of vertical.

14. *Pre-Launch Test*—When conducting research activities with unproven designs or methods, I will, when possible, determine their reliability through pre-launch tests. I will conduct launchings of unproven designs in complete isolation from persons not participating in the actual launching.

Fig. 5.2. Rocketry safety code. Used with permission of Estes Industries.

Chapter Six

The School Assembly

Preparing for the Assembly

A student-produced assembly program, just prior to the launch, is an excellent and rewarding experience for all. Middle school students can write their own script and elementary students can use the script provided in this chapter, if they desire to do so. The speeches are intentionally short to give every student an opportunity to speak and to save time allotted for the launch. Speeches can be divided between students so that all students can participate. Students often enjoy writing their own script for an upcoming assembly program. Writing a script is a great language activity extension.

To have a successful assembly program, keep in mind that many students may not want to participate. You can overcome this attitude by keeping speeches short. It is best if students do not take a written copy of their speech with them on stage, because this detracts from the spontaneity you hope to achieve. Holding a written copy also makes it difficult for them to demonstrate various experiments. However, the MC (Master of Ceremonies) should have a copy of the entire program, because he or she must know each part of the script in case a student is absent the day of the performance. Every student should give a speech, regardless of how short it might be.

After receiving permission from the principal and scheduling time in the auditorium, students can make invitations for their parents and the other classes to come to their assembly program and to watch the launch after the program. When their peers attend, the "rocketeers" attain a greater feeling of pride and accomplishment. Making invitations is also an opportunity to stimulate students' writing and art skills. If you are going to hold a drawing for a rocket (as suggested in the assembly script) be sure to advertise the drawing in the invitations to pique interest.

Place a chair for each student on the stage, and seat the students in the order in which they will be giving their speeches. This arrangement will save time and keep the program moving. After each student gives his or her speech, it is helpful if he or she leaves the stage by a back way and goes outside to the launching area designated prior to the program. However, if students have to cross in front of the audience to leave the stage, it is best if they remain on stage until the end of the assembly program.

Have the students present the assembly program without the teacher being visible. A student MC can keep the program moving, eliminating the need for a teacher to always be center-stage.

Here are some of the students' written remarks regarding their program:

"I was embarrassed when I did my speech. I couldn't reach the microphone, so I just said my speech."

"We put a program on the stage for launching rockets. My stepmom came to see me. Everyone in school came. It was fun saying my speech."

"I told my speech. Everybody in school saw me. I was happy when I gave my speech."

"I was nervous when I told my speech. It was fun."

"I called my grandma in Israel and told her how I said my speech for all the school. My grandma was very proud of me."

"The whole school was there and I was shy because I thought they would laugh at me. But they didn't. It was fun."

"My speech was a little short. My mom came in just in time to listen to my speech. I was happy when I said my speech because lots of people clapped."

"My speech was about how the first rockets were made by the Chinese. I wanted to just go through it and be over with it."

"I did my speech and somebody took a picture. I was excited when I gave my speech."

"When I gave my speech I felt great. Everyone clapped. My mom and dad came to see me. There were a lot of people there."

Sample Script for the Assembly Program

The sample script on pages 63-67 can be used for an assembly program as is or as the basis for a student-written script. The numbers used are merely to identify a different student for each of the speeches. If the class size demands more speaking parts, the speeches can be divided, or several students can assist each other. For more spontaneity, students should not read from the script during the actual presentation. If students cannot remember their speech, they should be encouraged to ad-lib.

Some class time must be devoted to preparing the props used in the program. Most of the props are taken directly from the activities. Students should be given time to practice their parts so they will feel confident during the assembly. Also, the script calls for an extra rocket to be given away to a student in a drawing. If you are going to do so, a student or students will have to be assigned to make the rocket.

Activities

———— Presenting a Student Assembly ————

Objective

To demonstrate the principles of rocketry to an audience of students.

Props Needed

Student 1: Bamboo stick

Student 2: Fire-arrow

Student 3: Large drawing of Wan-Hu's rocket chair

Student 4: Skateboard

Student 5: Balloon

Student 6: Fishing line and straw (attached to the stage prior to assembly), balloon, tape

Student 7: Rocket pinwheel (see activity 2.3)

Student 8: Rocket car (see activity 2.5)

Student 9: Glass milk bottle, matches, paper, hard-boiled egg

Student 10: Sink plunger, small student chair, water

Student 11: Model rocket

Student 12: Fishing line attached to a wall of the auditorium (but not to the stage; previously set-up), two-stage balloon rocket (see activity 1.1)

Student 13: Two paper rockets, one with fins and one without (see activity 3.2)

Student 14: Arrow

Student 15: Model rocket parachute, large drawing of Leonardo da Vinci's parachute

Student 16: Demonstration parachute made from a large garbage sack, tape, cord, and weight (made prior to the assembly)

Student 17: Helium-filled balloon with a postcard addressed to the school tied to it

Student 18: Decorated shoe box with names of students inside

Student 19: No prop needed

Student 20: Model rocket

Student 21: No prop needed

Student 22: No prop needed

Preparation

When preparing for the assembly program, students enjoy decorating a "space" shoe box. Have all the students in the different classes put their names into this box for a drawing at the assembly program. The student whose name is drawn is invited to the stage to receive a model rocket (already assembled) to launch with the rocketeers.

Besides the props, chairs, cassette, and microphone set-up, it is necessary to have two separate wires or fishing lines attached to one wall of the auditorium, to be used for the balloon demonstrations. Attach the other loose end of one of the lines to a point on the stage; this line should be taut. The end of the other fishing line should be on the stage but should be left loose; it will be attached during the program. The fishing lines have to be high enough so as not to interfere with the students.

The microphone should be near the prop table where the MC will be seated. If a student is absent, the MC can take over the speech.

Music

Music should be playing as students from the other classes enter the auditorium. Music helps set the mood for the program and also tends to calm students and counters the noise of other classes as they enter the auditorium. Play the theme from "2001: A Space Odyssey" or another popular science fiction film. When all are seated, the music should gradually fade out.

The Assembly Script

MC

We want to thank you for coming to watch our short program. After the program, with your teachers' permission, we will all go out to the yard to watch our rocket launching. Right now, we will get started with (*name of Student 1*) telling you about the beginning of rocketry.

Student 1

Since the beginning of time, people have looked to the stars and dreamed of traveling in space. We all know that this is now possible. Rockets came into being about one thousand years ago. It was the Chinese who made something like a rocket to be used for fireworks. I made a model of what it might have looked like. (*Hold up a bamboo tube.*) They filled a bamboo tube with some gunpowder and threw it into a fire so that there would be explosions.

Student 2

The bamboo tube the Chinese used would fly off in all directions. They experimented and soon attached the bamboo tube to an arrow and filled the tube with gunpowder. (*Show a bamboo tube attached to an arrow. Throw the arrow across the stage.*) The arrow guided the rocket. The Chinese used this fire-arrow to fight their wars.

Student 3

The Chinese say that there was a man called Wan-Hu. He sat in a chair that had two large kites attached to it, and 47 fire-arrow rockets fixed to the kites. I drew a picture of what it might have looked like. (*Hold up drawing of Wan-Hu and his rocket chair.*) When the fire-arrows were lit—Poof! All they saw was smoke. When the smoke had cleared, Wan-Hu was nowhere to be seen! The chair and Wan-Hu had been blown to pieces!

Student 4

More than 250 years ago, Sir Isaac Newton, an English scientist, stated the Laws of Motion. Rockets work because of his Third Law of Motion. He said that for every action there is an equal and opposite reaction. (*Show the skateboard.*) When I step on this skateboard (*step on skateboard*), it doesn't move. But when I push ahead on the skateboard and then jump off—my jumping off is the action but the skateboard travels backward. This is the opposite reaction. Watch! (*Push ahead on the skateboard and then jump off.*)

Student 5

See what happens when I blow up this balloon and let it go. (*Blow up balloon and let it go toward the audience.*) When the balloon is filled with air, the air on the inside pushes against the balloon's wall. The inward pressure is balanced against the outside pressure. But when I let go of the balloon, air escapes and the balloon goes in the opposite direction. This demonstration also shows Newton's Third Law of Motion.

Student 6

Another way to show how a rocket works is with a balloon. I will blow up this balloon and attach it to the straw on the fishing line we set up earlier. (*Blow up the balloon and attach it to the straw with tape.*) When I let go of the balloon, the air will escape and the backward push of the air inside the balloon will push the balloon forward. (*Let go of the balloon, which will travel along the wire.*) What you have seen is an example of Newton's Third Law of Motion. Rocket engines work in a similar way.

Student 7

Another way to demonstrate an opposite reaction is with the rocket pinwheel I made. (*Point to parts on the pinwheel as it is explained.*) I used a pencil, a pin, a balloon, tape, and a flexible soda straw. I put the end of the balloon over the end of the straw and taped it. Then I found the balance point on the straw and put a pin through it and into the eraser of the pencil. Watch as I blow up the balloon and let it go. (*Blow through the straw to fill the balloon. Let go of the straw.*) Notice how the balloon and the straw spin around the pin. This, too, shows the action-reaction rule.

Student 8

I made a rocket car, which also demonstrates Newton's Third Law of Motion. (*Show the rocket car while explaining how it was made.*) I used four pins to attach Styrofoam wheels to a Styrofoam meat tray. I taped a balloon to the end of this straw and taped the straw to this Styrofoam. Watch what happens when I blow up the balloon and pinch the straw so no air can escape. (*Blow up the balloon on the straw. Pinch the end of the straw.*) Now see what happens when I let go of the straw. (*Let go of the straw.*) The escaping air from the balloon is the action and the reaction is my car moving ahead.

Student 9

I can also demonstrate to you Newton's Third Law of Motion. I'll show you what happens when there is a difference in air pressure creating the action and opposite reaction. Watch what happens when we put some burning paper into this glass milk bottle and place a peeled hard-boiled egg on top. (*The teacher or adult assistant lights the paper and puts it inside the bottle. The student quickly places the egg on the opening of the bottle.*) The burning paper used up some of the oxygen from the air inside the bottle and, because of this, there was less air pressure. The air pressure on the outside of the bottle was then greater, so it pushed the egg into the bottle.

Student 10

You can also see the effect of differences in air pressure with this plunger. I'll put a little water on the rubber cup. (*Pour water around the rim of the plunger.*) Now I'll push the plunger onto this chair. (*Press the plunger on the chair. Lift the chair.*) I can lift the chair with the plunger because the air pressure outside the plunger is greater than the air pressure inside the plunger, causing the plunger to stick to the chair.

Student 11

(*Hold rocket made in class.*) The same holds true for a rocket. The rocket pushes on the gas in a rocket and the gas in turn pushes on the rocket. The gas inside the rocket escapes from the rocket, releasing pressure, and the rocket goes up.

Student 12

To demonstrate the effect of different stages on a rocket, I have used these two balloons. They are both filled with air. (*Show the balloons with the attached straws as in the balloon staging experiment.*) I will slip this fish line through both straws. (*Slip the loose fishing line through the straws, as in activity 1.1. Have another student hold the fishing line taut.*) Let's have a countdown! (*Everyone in the audience and the students on the stage count down to blast-off. Then let go of the balloon to release the air from the second balloon.*) This is like rocket staging. When the lower stage has released its load of propellants, the second stage can reach higher altitudes.

Student 13

For a model rocket to be stable in its flight, it needs fins. (*Hold model rocket and point to the fins.*) I have a paper rocket that does not have fins on it. Notice what happens when I throw it. (*Throw the paper rocket without fins.*) I made this rocket, just like the one I threw, but it has fins. (*Point to the fins on the paper rocket.*) Now notice what happens when I throw this rocket. (*Throw the paper rocket with fins.*) It flies straight.

Student 14

I'll show you why fins are necessary for a straight flight. As you all know, an arrow has feathers. (*Hold up an arrow.*) The feathers on the arrow act like the fins on our model rocket. If the arrow didn't have feathers, it wouldn't fly straight. Notice what happens when I throw this arrow. (*Throw the arrow.*)

Student 15

Our model rockets have parachutes, which prevent them from falling too fast to the ground. (*Show the model rocket parachute.*) It was Leonardo da Vinci who designed the first parachute. It doesn't look like the parachutes we use now. He called his parachute a "tent roof." This is a picture of the first parachute. (*Show the enlarged drawing of the first parachute.*)

Student 16

I will show you an example of a parachute. (*While talking, show and point to parts on the garbage sack.*) In class, I took a garbage sack and cut a large hexagon out of it. I attached some shroud lines to it and tied a weight where the shroud lines come together. When I throw this parachute, the air resistance fills the parachute and prevents it from falling too fast. (*Throw parachute across the stage.*)

Student 17

I have this helium-filled balloon with a postcard tied to it. (*Point to postcard.*) On the postcard we have the address of our school, so that if anyone finds the balloon and mails the postcard back to us, we will know where it landed.

Student 18

Everyone at school recognizes this box. (*Hold up space shoe box.*) Most of you have your name in it. We will now draw the name of the student who will be given a rocket to keep and to launch the rocket with our class.

Student 19

I'll draw the name of the lucky person. (*Draws name from the box. Reads the name.*) Will (*name of student*) please come up.

Student 20

(*Hands student the rocket.*) Here is your rocket. I'll take you out to the launching site. (*Both students leave the stage to go to the launching site.*)

Student 21

There are safety rules to follow when launching rockets. We have studied the rules and will follow all safety rules. Rockets can only be launched under the supervision of an adult. To launch our rockets, we had to get permission from the fire department.

Student 22

Please remember that when you go out, you are to stay with your class. No one is to chase our rockets when they float to the ground. The only one who is to catch the rocket is the one who launched it. It is very important to remember that no one is to be near the launch pad except the one who is launching the rocket. Please, stay with your class.

MC

This concludes our program. We hope you have enjoyed it. If you want to watch the launching of our rockets, please go with your teacher to our launch site. Thank you.

Chapter Seven

Blast Off!

The rocket launch is the culmination of your rocketry activities. You may have launched some test flights before this point. If so, your students will know what to expect. If not, prior to the launch, review the sequence of a rocket flight (fig. 7.1). This is the day students have been waiting for, so have fun!

A Successful Launch

Expect the rocketeers to be excited on the day of the assembly and launch. Prior to the launch or assembly program, standards for behavior need to have been established. Students need to know that out-of-control behavior is unacceptable. It is helpful if the students believe they will be excluded from the launch if they misbehave. Because they may possibly launch their rockets more than one time, students also can be told that they will not be able to launch again if they are unruly during the launch. Generally, students are so focused on rocket launching that there is seldom any misbehavior.

If an assembly program is planned, know that students will always be on their best behavior during the program. Having parents and their peers at the program gives students the incentive to be well behaved.

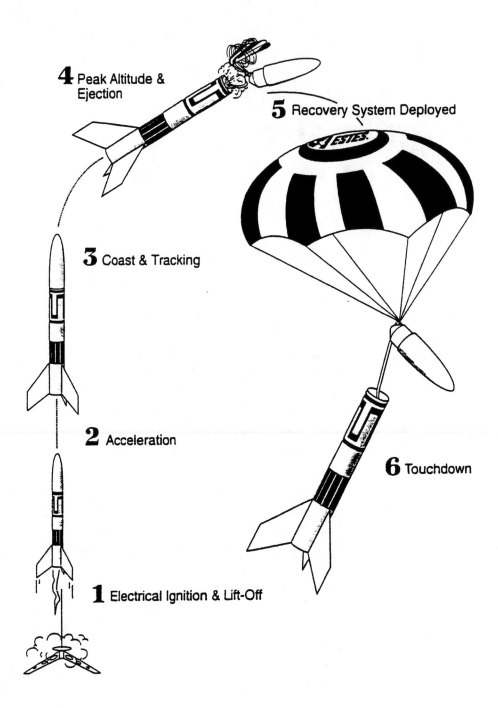

Fig. 7.1. Rocket flight sequence. Used with permission of Estes Industries.

Students enjoy the launch more if they are active participants in the preparation for the actual launch. Different team assignments will not only give students the responsibility for the success of their launch but also aids the teacher in having an orderly launch.

Several students should be assigned to make certain that the tables needed for supplies and repair are at the launch site. There is no necessity for chairs; however, if the teacher in charge of the launch prefers to sit on a chair, a student can bring a chair to the launch site. I have found that it is best to sit on the ground during the launch.

Regardless of the age of students who may want to be in charge of the motors and igniters, it is best for the teacher to stay in charge. It is the final responsibility of the teacher to account for all the motors and igniters.

One team can check the individual rockets to be sure they are packed and have motors installed and check the rocket boxes to make certain that all have numbers indicating the launch order.

A recording team can be assigned to time and track the rockets. The team should have a list of the rocketeers in the order that they will be launching their rockets. This checklist makes it easy to record the timing and tracking information. This team is also responsible for taking charge of the stop watch and tracking device.

The student in charge of checking off the rocketeers as they launch their rockets should be seated by the teacher giving out the motors for the second launch. The checker will immediately know who has already launched a second rocket and prevent a third motor from being given to a student until everyone has had two launches. The same method can be used if there are going to be more than two launches. With a large class, though, there is generally only time for two launches.

Before the assembly program, if given, each student should go to the launch site and place his or her launch in numerical order. These rockets can be placed on a table for that purpose or, preferably, on the ground where the students will be sitting.

Almost ready to launch.

Considering the trajectory of the model rockets, a team should be selected to make certain that all obstacles are removed from the launch and recovery area. This team must also inform all teachers who will be watching the launch to bring chairs for their students to the launch site. This extra measure will help prevent students from chasing the rockets when they fall to the ground. Even though they have been told that only the student who launched the rocket is to chase it, some other students invariably try to catch the rocket.

Typically, the students observing the launch will start a countdown as soon as the rocket is placed on the launch rod, when the student is holding the electrical igniter, or when the safety key is put in the controller. Avoid this by putting one student in charge of the countdown. The rocketeer can then signal the start of the countdown when ready. In this way, the student who is about to launch his or her rocket does not become overly excited trying to meet the countdown from the other students. The next student to launch a rocket should be nearby and ready to go to save time between launches.

After the launches are over, have the different teams return all the equipment to the classroom, including the launch pad, launch controller, clipboards, tracking device, stop watch, repair materials, and the tables. The teacher and assistant are responsible for the extra motors, igniters, and safety keys. A team should be assigned for the final clean up of the launch site, such as the removal of burned out igniters and motors as well as wadding that has been blown out of the rocket. Each student is responsible for removing his or her own rocket and storage box. At times, though, students leave their rocket storage boxes at the site, so these too have to be removed. School personnel will be grateful that the rocketeers cleaned up the area.

Blast off!

Catching the rocket on descent.

For safety reasons, an assistant (adult) should place the safety cap on the top of the launch rod after each launch. This step will prevent someone from accidentally getting hurt on the launch rod. Only after the student has retrieved his or her rocket is the cap removed and the next student allowed to slide his or her rocket onto the launch rod. When the teacher or other assistant (adult) puts the safety key back into the electrical controller, the student is ready to launch.

Occasionally there will be a misfire: The rocket does not launch. The first thing to do is to hold the button down on the controller for a few seconds because it may be caused by a weak battery. If it still does not ignite, remove the safety key and, after waiting for at least a minute, approach the launch pad to check other possible causes for the misfire.

At the launch pad, put the safety cap back on the launch rod. Check the clips that attach the electrical system to the igniter. They may be making poor contact by touching metal or they may be coated with exhaust. This problem can be easily and quickly remedied by using a small nail file or sandpaper to clean them. If the igniter has fallen out of the motor, use the plugs that come with the igniters to hold them in place. Remove the launch rod safety cap when you are ready to launch.

The second launch can be hectic unless students know ahead of time what to expect. Because some rocketeers will take more time to repack their rockets or, hopefully not, make repairs on their rockets, there may be no particular order to the launches.

Launch Checklist

Use the launch checklist (fig. 7.2) to organize your materials for the launch. If you find you need additional items, add them to your checklist.

Launch Checklist

Class/Number of students _____

Launch Date _____

Launch Time _____

- ☐ Launch pad
- ☐ Launch rod and safety cap
- ☐ Electric launch controller and batteries
- ☐ Safety key for the controller
- ☐ Motors. Number needed: _____ (Number of students times number of launches)
- ☐ Igniters
- ☐ Wadding
- ☐ Talcum powder (for the parachutes)
- ☐ Masking tape
- ☐ Cellophane tape
- ☐ Needle-nose pliers (to remove burned out motors stuck in mounts)
- ☐ Tracking device
- ☐ Stop watch
- ☐ Two clipboards for the tracking and timing operators
- ☐ Paper and pencils
- ☐ Rocket launch check sheet (for recording each launch to prevent excess launches by individuals)
- ☐ Optional: binoculars, camera

DON'T FORGET THE ROCKETS!

Fig. 7.2. Launch checklist.

Altitude Tracking

Students always want to know how high their rockets flew. A tracking device is required to calculate a rocket's altitude. Commercial altitude tracking devices can be purchased or students can make their own tracking devices. Activity 7.1 provides an easy alternative to purchasing a tracking device. With an understanding of the mathematics involved, they can calculate the actual flight altitudes.

Using the tracking device takes some practice. The calculations themselves are fairly simple. Activity 7.2 offers instructions and an example. It is important that students practice with their sighting tube prior to launching their rockets. Several different practice objects should be used with the tracking device—such as street lights, flagpoles, buildings, and trees—prior to tracking an actual launch.

Activities

7.1 Making a Tracking Device

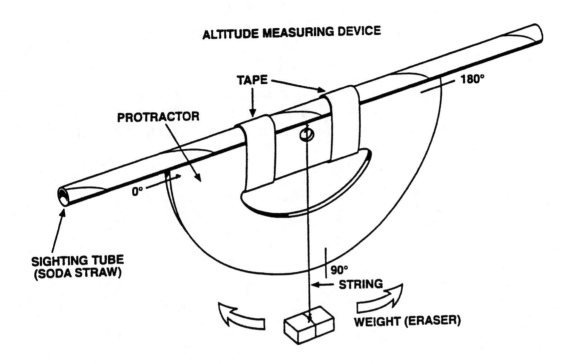

ALTITUDE MEASURING DEVICE

Fig. 7.3. A simple tracking device.

Objective

To make an altitude tracking device to calculate how high their rockets flew.

Materials

Large diameter soda straw
20-centimeter length of string
Protractor
Eraser
Tape

Procedure

1. Tape the straw across the top of the protractor, as shown in figure 7.3.
2. Tie the string around the eraser.
3. Slip the other end of the string under and around the straw.
4. Tie the string to itself and tape it to the back of the protractor.

Explanation

The straw on the protractor acts as a sighting tube. The string crosses the protractor and shows the angle needed to determine the altitude. Activity 7.2 gives detailed instructions on how to calculate altitude.

7.2 Using a Tracking Device

Objective

To determine a rocket's altitude using a tracking device.

Materials

Using simple trigonometry to determine the altitude a rocket reaches in flight is a challenging math activity. The mathematical formula for altitude tracking is altitude equals baseline times tangent of angular distance, illustrated by the following formula:

RL = LT x tan$\angle a$

RL = the peak altitude of the rocket

LT = the baseline, i.e., the distance between the launch pad and the tracking station

$\angle a$ = angular distance, the elevation angle as measured by the tracking operator

For convenience, a table of tangents (see appendix A) is provided to find the tangent of the angular distance.

Prior to launching, measure the distance from the launching pad to the tracking station. The baseline distance should be recorded for later use.

The student(s) doing the tracking should be at the tracking station and focus the sighting tube on the rocket as it ascends. When the rocket reaches apogee (its highest point), the string attached to the protractor should be fixed in its position on the protractor. Remind students that the angles of a triangle added together equal 180 degrees. The angular distance is found by subtracting 90 degrees from the protractor reading. Record this actual angular distance. Also, the height of the student doing the tracking has to be taken into consideration. The height of the student at eye level will have to be added to the final altitude calculation.

Here's an example: Assume that the distance between the launching pad and the tracking station is 500 feet and the angular distance is 30 degrees (90 degrees - 60 degrees [the reading on the protractor] = 30 degrees). The tangent of the angular distance, derived from the table, is .58.

The data from this example will look like this:

Baseline (*LT*): 500 feet
Angular distance (*a*): 30 degrees
Tangent of angular distance (*tan∠a*): .58

With this data the formula can be completed:

Altitude = baseline x tangent of angular distance
Height = 500 feet x .58
Height = 290 feet

Now add the height of the student at eye level (5 feet) to the calculated height. The altitude the rocket reached is 295 feet.

Post-Launch Activities

Math Activities

After students have collected the data, the actual altitude achieved by the rocket can be calculated using the altitude tracking formula stated above. Students will first want to know whose rocket went highest. Other activities, though, can be done using the information recorded at the launch.

Students will be able to find the mean of the altitudes reached by the rockets. Calculating the median and mode of the launchings is another excellent math activity. Analyzing the difference between the highest altitude reached by a rocket and the lowest, students can calculate the range for their set of data.

The same calculations can be done using the flight time data recorded by the time keeper. Students can then incorporate both sets of data to answer such questions as: What was the relationship between flight time and altitude reached? Was the rocket with the longest flight time also the highest? Why or why not? Students will be highly motivated to complete these math activities because they are relevant to their rocket experience.

Writing About the Experience

Have the rocketeers write about their rocketry experiences. Collect and assemble the compositions into a class book. If photos were taken showing the students constructing their rockets, putting on the assembly program, or launching their rockets, include these in the book. The rocketeers will enjoy sharing their compositions with the other classes and displaying them at the school office. The class book, including the photos, can be photocopied to give each student a book. This book with stories and pictures of the launch will be a treasured keepsake for all the rocketeers (and their teacher).

To quote from students' written compositions from a special education class:

"Making the rocket, and especially launching it, was the most fun thing I ever did."

"I was excited when I launched my rocket. I caught my rocket the first time, but I didn't catch it the second time."

"My rocket blast off and the parachute came out. Then I ran and caught it. It was real fun."

"My aunt and uncle came and watched me launch my rocket. I had fun."

"We launched our rockets. They went all the way up high. I caught my rocket the second time and then I put my new engine in. I had fun."

"When I was going to launch my rocket, it was so scary. But it was fun. When it came down, I was supposed to get it, but I dropped it."

"All the kids counted 5-4-3-2-1 Blast-off! Everyone yelled and clapped when I caught my rocket. I sure had fun when I launched my rocket."

"I felt scared that my rocket wouldn't launch. I was saying to myself to please, please launch. It launched. Everyone yelled and clapped for me."

Appendixes

Appendix A

Table of Tangents

Angle	Tan.	Angle	Tan.	Angle	Tan.
1°	.02	28°	.53	55°	1.43
2	.03	29	.55	56	1.48
3	.05	30	.58	57	1.54
4	.07	31	.60	58	1.60
5	.09	32	.62	59	1.66
6	.11	33	.65	60	1.73
7	.12	34	.67	61	1.80
8	.14	35	.70	62	1.88
9	.16	36	.73	63	1.96
10	.18	37	.75	64	2.05
11	.19	38	.78	65	2.14
12	.21	39	.81	66	2.25
13	.23	40	.84	67	2.36
14	.25	41	.87	68	2.48
15	.27	42	.90	69	2.61
16	.29	43	.93	70	2.75
17	.31	44	.97	71	2.90
18	.32	45	1.00	72	3.08
19	.34	46	1.04	73	3.27
20	.36	47	1.07	74	3.49
21	.38	48	1.11	75	3.73
22	.40	49	1.15	76	4.01
23	.42	50	1.19	77	4.33
24	.45	51	1.23	78	4.70
25	.47	52	1.28	79	5.14
26	.49	53	1.33	80	5.67
27	.51	54	1.38		

Appendix B

English-Metric Conversions

Length

1 inch = 2.54 centimeters

1 foot = 0.304 meters

1 yard = 0.914 meters

1 statute mile (5280 feet) = 1.609 kilometers

1 centimeter = 0.393 inches

1 meter = 3.28 feet

1 meter = 1.093 yards

1 kilometer = 0.62 statute miles

Capacity/Volume

1 cubic inch = 16.387 cubic centimeters

1 cubic foot = 0.028 cubic meters

1 cubic yard = 0.765 cubic meters

1 pint = 0.473 liters

1 quart = 0.946 liters

1 gallon = 3.785 liters

1 cubic centimeter = 0.061 cubic inches

1 cubic meter = 35.289 cubic feet

1 cubic meter = 1.307 cubic yards

1 liter (1,000 cc) = 0.035 cubic feet

1 liter = 1.057 quarts

1 liter = 2.114 pints

Weight

1 ounce = 28.349 grams

1 pound = 0.454 kilograms

1 kilogram = 2.205 pounds

Conversions (Approximate)

Miles to kilometers: Multiply by 8 and divide by 5, or multiply by 1.6.

Kilometers to miles: Multiply by 5 and divide by 8, or multiply by .625.

Appendix C

Rocketry Certificates

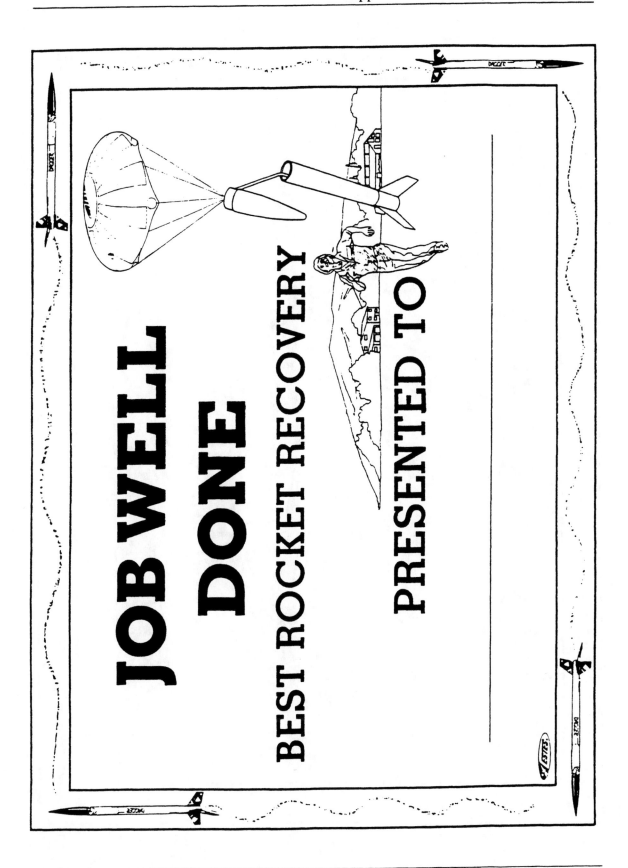

JOB WELL DONE

BEST ROCKET RECOVERY

PRESENTED TO

MOST LIKELY TO BECOME AN EXPERT ROCKETEER

HIGH FLYING ROCKET AWARD

PRESENTED TO

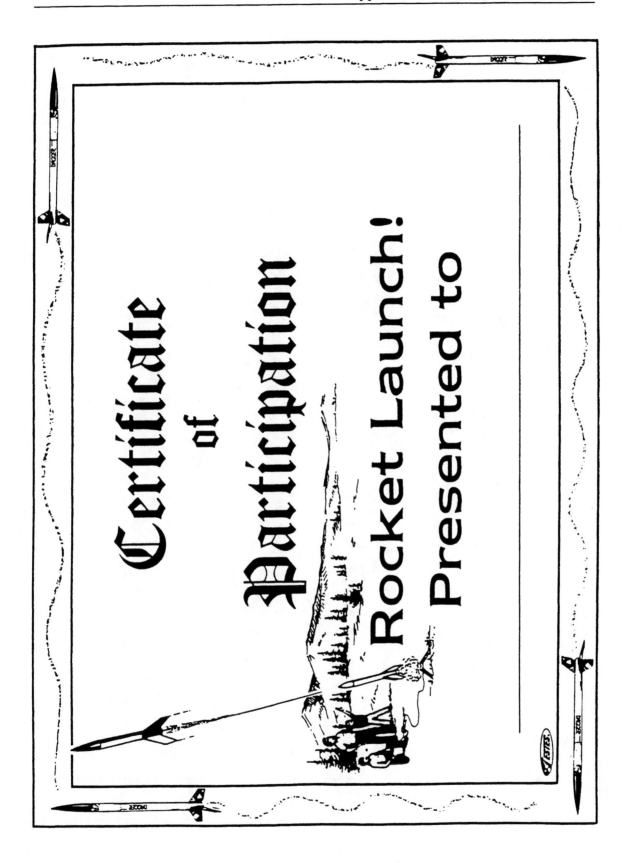

Certificate
of
Participation

Rocket Launch!

Presented to

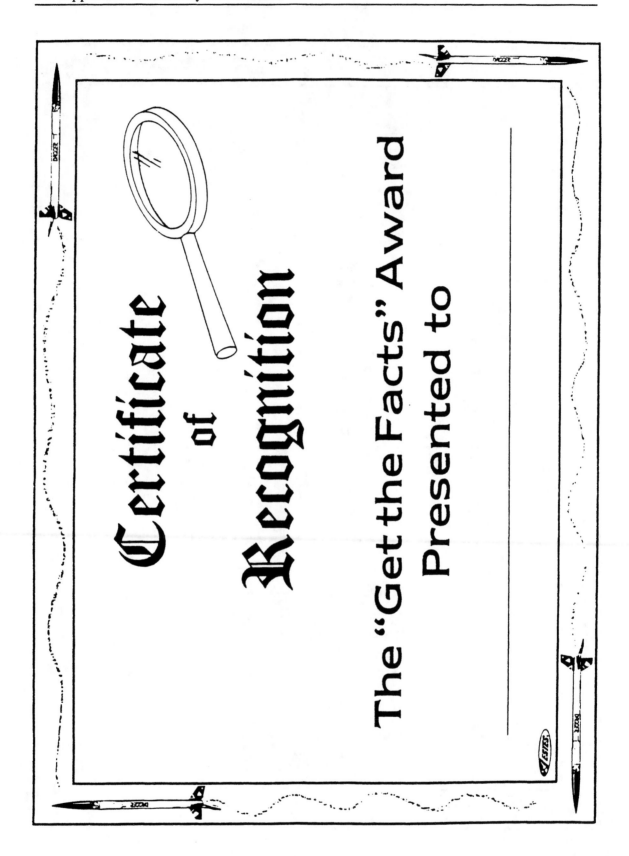

Certificate of Recognition

The "Get the Facts" Award

Presented to

_____

Certificate of Mathematics Skills

Good Guesser Award

Presented to

For Excellence in Estimating

Glossary

acceleration. The increase of speed or velocity of an object.

action. A force (push or pull) acting on an object.

active controls. Devices on a rocket that move (i.e., are active) to control the rocket's direction in flight.

air pressure. The force of air as it presses down and against all sides of an object. Atmospheric pressure at sea level is 14.7 pounds per square inch (1.036 kilograms per square centimeter).

air resistance. The resistance of the air to anything moving against it.

altitude. Elevation above sea level; also refers to the height of an object above ground level (such as a model rocket in flight).

apogee. The highest point in a model rocket's flight; also the greatest distance an object (such as a satellite) reaches from the body it is orbiting.

case. The body of a solid-propellant rocket that holds the propellant.

center of mass (CM). The point in an object about which the object's mass is centered.

center of pressure (CP). The point in an object about which the object's surface area is centered.

chamber. A cavity inside a rocket where propellants burn.

combustion chamber. *See* chamber.

drag. Friction forces in the atmosphere that drag on a rocket to slow its flight.

escape velocity. The velocity an object must reach to escape the pull of Earth's gravity.

fins. Wings at the lower end of a rocket that are used to stabilize the rocket in flight.

fuel. The chemical that combines with an oxidizer to burn and produce thrust.

gantry. A platform from which a rocket is launched.

gravity. A fundamental physical force responsible for the attraction of objects, e.g., the Earth and moon; also, the attraction of the Earth for objects near its surface.

igniter. A device that ignites a rocket's engine(s).

insulation. A coating that protects the case and nozzle of a rocket from intense heat.

launch. Send off.

launch controller. A device that sends electricity to start the igniter.

launch lug. A round tube attached to the body of a model rocket that is slipped over the launch rod to guide the rocket during the first few feet of flight.

launch pad. A device that holds the rocket off the ground for launching.

launch rod. A wire-like device on the launch pad that guides the rocket for its first few feet of flight.

liquid propellant. Rocket propellants in liquid form.

mass. The amount of matter contained within an object.

motion. Movement of an object in relation to its surroundings.

movable fins. Rocket fins that can move to stabilize a rocket's flight.

nose cone. The cone-shaped front end of a rocket.

nozzle. A bell-shaped opening at the lower end of a rocket through which a stream of hot gases is directed outward.

oxidizer. A chemical containing oxygen compounds that permits rocket fuel to burn both in the atmosphere and in the vacuum of space.

passive controls. Stationary devices, such as fixed fins, that stabilize a rocket in flight.

payload. The cargo carried by a rocket.

propellant. A mixture of fuel and oxidizer that burns to produce rocket thrust.

reaction. A movement in the opposite direction from the imposition of an action.

rest. The absence of movement of an object in relation to its surroundings.

solid propellant. Rocket fuel and oxidizer in solid form.

stages. Two or more rockets stacked on top of each other to allow the rocket to reach higher altitudes or have a greater payload capacity.

throat. The narrow opening of a rocket nozzle.

thrust. A forward push.

tracking. Following the course of a rocket flight.

tracking device. A device to follow the flight of a model rocket and used to help calculate the highest altitude reached.

unbalanced force. A force that is not countered by another force in the opposite direction.

wadding. Flame-resistant tissue packed between the rocket motor and the parachute to prevent burning upon ejection.

Resources

Books

Alway, Peter. *Rockets of the World: A Modeler's Guide.* Ann Arbor, MI: Saturn Press, 1993.

Anzovin, Steven. *Our Future in Space.* New York: H. W. Wilson, 1991.

Banks, Michael A. *Advanced Model Rocketry.* Milwaukee, WI: Kalmbach, 1985.

————. *Countdown: The Complete Guide to Model Rocketry.* Blue Ridge Summit, PA: TAB Books, 1985

Banks, Michael A. and Robert L. Cannon. *The Rocket Book: A Guide to Building & Launching Model Rockets for Teachers & Students of the Space Age.* Englewood Cliffs, NJ: Prentice-Hall, 1985.

Cannon, Robert L. and Michael A. Banks. *The Rocket Book.* Englewood Cliffs, NJ: Prentice-Hall, 1985.

Estes Industries. *Estes Manual.* Penrose, CO: Estes Industries, 1985.

Hartsfield, John W. and Kendra J. Hartsfield. *Human Spaceflight: Activities for the Intermediate and Junior High Student.* Cleveland, OH: National Aeronautics and Space Administration, 1985.

Hujsak, Edward. *The Future of U.S. Rocketry.* San Diego, CA: San Diego Publishing, 1994.

Humphrey, B. J. *A Hundred Ways to Save on Model Rocket Building.* Claremont, CA: California Rocketry, Division of U.S. Rocketry, 1977.

Jennings, Terry. *Flying & Gliding.* Chatham, NJ: Raintree Steck-Vaughn, 1995.

Kennedy, Gregory P. *Rockets, Missiles & Spacecraft of the National Air & Space Museum.* Washington, DC: Smithsonian Institution, 1983.

Mandell, Gordon K. *Topics in Advanced Model Rocketry.* Cambridge: MIT Press, 1973.

Millspaugh, Ben. *Aviation and Space Science Projects.* Rockford, IL: TAB Books, 1991.

National Aeronautics and Space Administration. *All Aboard for Space*. Kennedy Space Center, FL: NASA, 1992.

————. *Rockets*. Washington, DC: NASA, 1993.

Pratt, Douglas R. *Basics of Model Rocketry* (2nd ed.). Milwaukee, WI: Kalmbach, 1995.

Ray, Robert D. and Joan Klingel Ray. *Integrating Aerospace Science into the Curriculum*. Englewood, CO: Libraries Unlimited, 1992.

Schall, William E. *Countdown: Mathematics and Model Rocketry*. Penrose, CO: Estes Industries, 1981.

Stine, G. Harry. *Handbook of Model Rocketry* (6th ed.). New York: John Wiley Sons, 1994.

Walter, William J. *Space Age*. New York: Random House, 1994.

Winter, Frank H. *The First Golden Age of Rocketry: Congreve & Hale Rockets of the Nineteenth Century*. Washington, DC: Smithsonian Institution, 1990.

Juvenile Literature

Armstrong, Jennifer. *Wan Hu Is in the Stars*. New York: Tambourine, 1995.

Asimov, Isaac. *Rockets, Probes & Satellites*. Milwaukee, WI: Gareth Stevens, 1988.

Baird, Anne. *The U.S. Space Camp Book of Rockets*. New York: William Morrow, 1994.

Branley, Franklyn M. *Rockets & Satellites*. New York: HarperCollins Children's Books, 1987.

Goodwain, Harold L. *All About Rockets & Space Flight*. New York: Random House Books for Young Readers, 1970.

Lampton, Christopher. *Rocketry from Goddard to Space Travel*. New York: Franklin Watts, 1988.

Mauer, Richard. *Rocket! How a Toy Launched the Space Age*. New York: Crown Books for Young Readers, 1995.

Myring. *Rockets and Spaceflight*. Tulsa, OK: Educational Development, 1982.

Streissguth, Tom. *Rocket Man: The Story of Robert Goddard*. Minneapolis, MN: Lerner, 1995.

Vogt, Gregory. *Model Rockets*. New York: Franklin Watts, 1982.

Magazine Articles

Fitzsimmons, Charles P. "Model Rockets and Microchips." *Science Teacher* 53, no. 2 (February 1986): 42-44.

Hawthorne, Monica and Gerry Saunders. "It's Launchtime!" *Science and Children* 30, no. 55 (February 1993): 17-19, 39.

Mirus, Edward A., Jr. "Microcomputers, Model Rockets, and Race Cars." *American Annals of the Deaf* 130 (November 1985): 431-35.

Rogis, Jeanne A. "Soaring with Aviation Activities." *Science Scope* 15 (October 1991): 14-17.

Sneider, Cary. "Learning to Control Variables with Model Rockets." *Science Education* 68 (July 1984): 465-68.

Winemiller, Jake. "The Rocket Project. 1991." *Science Scope* 15 (October 1991): 18-22

Magazines

High Power Rocketry
Tripoli Rocketry Association, Inc.
P.O. Box 96
Orem, UT 84059-0096

Sport Rocketry Magazine
National Association of Rocketry Headquarters
P.O. Box 177
Altoona, WI 54720

Associations

National Association of Rocketry (NAR)
P.O. Box 177
Altoona, WI 54720
(715) 882-1946
Telefax: #15 (715) 832-6432
Web site address http://www.nar.org

Tripoli Rocketry Association, Inc. (TRA)
P.O. Box 4075
St. Petersburg, FL 33743-0475
Tripoli Rocketry Association has many regional groups that can be contacted.

Index

About the Author

Lee Brattland Nielsen graduated from the University of Minnesota and continued her studies at the University of Florida, California State University, California Lutheran University, and the University of California.

She has taught in California for many years and is currently a Resource Specialist Teacher in special education in the Los Angeles Unified School District. She also taught education courses at California Lutheran University. Her teaching background includes working as a Resource Specialist in Dade County Public Schools in Florida.

Prior to teaching in Dade County, she was Women's Program Director at radio station WBAY in Coral Gables, Florida. She later became the program director for Dade County's first educational broadcasting station, WTHS, for Dade County Public Schools in Miami.

She has been incorporating model rocketry as a thematic unit in her classes since 1980.

from Teacher Ideas Press

INTEGRATING AEROSPACE SCIENCE INTO THE CURRICULUM: K–12
Robert D. Ray and Joan Klingel Ray

Demystify space with substantive information and hands-on activities that integrate space science with other curriculuar areas. **Grades K–12**.
Gifted Treasury Series; Jerry D. Flack, Ed.
xxi, 191p. 8½x11 paper ISBN 0-87287-924-0

SIMPLE MACHINES MADE SIMPLE
Ralph E. St. Andre

Present scientific principles and simple mechanics through hands-on cooperative learning activities that use *inexpensive* materials (e.g., tape, paper clips). **Grades 3–8**.
xix, 150p. 8½x11 paper ISBN 1-56308-104-0

INTERMEDIATE SCIENCE THROUGH CHILDREN'S LITERATURE: Over Land and Sea
Carol M. Butzow and John W. Butzow

Focusing on earth and environmental science themes and activities, each chapter centers on a work of literature and provides hands-on and discovery activities that implement scientific concepts. **Grades 4–7**.
xxv, 193p. 8½x11 paper ISBN 0-87287-946-1

EXPLORATIONS IN BACKYARD BIOLOGY: Drawing on Nature in the Classroom, Grades 4–6
R. Gary Raham

Discover life science adventures in your own backyard (or school yard)! Exciting classroom and field activities give students the opportunity for hands-on exploration. Using drawing and writing skills, they record their experiences in a Naturalist's Notebook, which encourages further discoveries. **Grades 4–6**.
xix, 204p. 8½x11 paper ISBN 1-56308-254-3

THE WORLD'S REGIONS AND WEATHER: Linking Fiction to Nonfiction
Phyllis J. Perry

Use the power of fiction and the imagination to draw students into the world of climate and weather. **Grades 5–9**.
Literature Bridges to Science Series
xvi, 157p. 8½x11 paper ISBN 1-56308-338-8

MARVELS OF SCIENCE: 50 Fascinating 5-Minute Reads
Kendall Haven

Ideal for both read-alouds and reading assignments, these 50 short stories take just minutes to read but amply illustrate scientific principles and the evolution of science through history. **Grades 3 and up**.
xxii, 238p. paper ISBN 1-56308-159-8

GREAT MOMENTS IN SCIENCE: Experiments and Readers Theatre
Kendall Haven

Significant moments and characters in the history of Western science come to life in 12 scripts that are linked with student experiments. These parallel or simulate the actual experiments in the stories, so that students can discover and learn the concepts for themselves. **Grades 4–9**.
xii, 227p. 8½x11 paper ISBN 1-56308-355-8

CIRCUIT SENSE FOR ELEMENTARY TEACHERS AND STUDENTS:
Understanding and Building Simple Logic Circuits
Janaye Matteson Houghton and Robert S. Houghton

Your classroom will be literally buzzing, flashing, and whirring with the simple and affordable activities generated by this handbook! **Grades K–6**.
xi, 65p. 8½x11 paper ISBN 1-56308-149-0

For a FREE catalog, or to order any of our titles, please contact:
Teacher Ideas Press • Dept. B22 • P.O. Box 6633 • Englewood, CO 80155-6633
1-800-237-6124, ext. 1 • Fax: 303-220-8843 • E-Mail: lu-books@lu.com